DEDICATED TO
MY PARTNER, BIJOU O'KEEFE.

Greatly appreciated was assistance from the wisest and bravest of cultural warriors:
Christophe Bourseiller, Nicole Canet, Alexandre Dupouy, Nina Hartley, Ira Levine, and Jean-Marie Pradier.

HORIZONTAL COLLABORATION

THE EROTIC WORLD OF PARIS, 1920–1946

MEL GORDON

FERAL HOUSE

PREFACE

||||||||||||||||||||||||||||||||||||||||||||||||||||||||||||||||||||||||||||||||||||||||||||||||||||||||||||||||||||||||||||||||||||||||||||||||||

On December 4th, 2007, a ten-story-tall "X" beamed across one of the towering façades of the Bibliothèque Nationale de France. The elegantly designed fuchsia-pink letter stood for Pornography. It signaled the inauguration of an exhibition devoted to the hidden erotic archive in the French national library. This celebrated collection, formerly restricted to reputable scholars of French culture and erotica, was known as *L'Enfer de la Bibliothèque*, or the Library's Cabinet of Hell. Dignitaries, politicians, and academics quaffed Champagne as they viewed the forbidden art and publications that spanned two-and-a-half centuries. The BnF bookstore shelves sagged with oversized reprints of formerly banned literary anthologies and obscene pictorial albums. Thin red curtains comically shielded the most explicit items.

Over the next three months, tens of thousands of Parisians paid ten euros to gawk at the shockingly transgressive imagery and licentious silent film clips that the Bibliothèque placed in glass cases or projected across framed movie screens. Only in Paris, local journalists enthused, would this massive display of antiquated and contemporary pornography be considered an authentic cultural phenomenon and expression of the city's not so secretive past and proud no-holds-barred distinctiveness.

For the most part, the municipal show was a salute to Erotic Paris and its aesthetization of all things sexual that reached an apogee during the 1920s and 1930s. Suddenly the discarded prurient junk and naughty ephemera from back-alley Montmartre and beyond were accorded a place of honor in

ABOVE: Cover of *L'Enfer de la Bibliothèque* Catalog (2007)

OPPOSITE: Vald'Es, "Dawn in Montmartre and He Thinks That Still He Can Remember His Name!" 1930

the underground history of the twentieth century. Establishment Paris was reflecting upon and then heralding its subversive past. The basement doors of the Bibliothèque had not only been unbolted but the salacious materials inside were dusted off for new and thoughtful deliberation. Commercialized sex was embraced yet again as a requisite component of interwar Paris and its amoral attractions.

OPPOSITE: Léon Bonnotte, *When the "Prisoners" Escape, or the Matrons of Éphèse-City,* 1928

Horizontal Collaboration: the Erotic World of Paris, 1920–1946 is one author's attempt to recover and evaluate a specific place and time of sex culture. The book encompasses the periods of the Jazz Age, Depression, World War and Occupation, Liberation, and Postwar Stability. It concludes with the shuttering of the licensed brothels in 1946, which some Parisian intellectuals thought was the final "destruction of French civilization" and its hedonistic exceptionalism.

The term "Horizontal Collaboration" normally refers to the voluntary sexual liaisons between French civilians and their German occupiers from 1940 to 1944. These were extremely widespread and included both individual wartime relationships and mercantile contacts. As the Allied armies swept across the French countryside, thousands of young women — and some men — were implicated for their intimate acquaintances with the enemy and then savagely punished by the authorities or by vigilante crowds. The enormity of the "Horizontal Collaboration" was a source of deep national shame and disgrace for an entire generation.

This book, however, redefines the historically pejorative idiom to mean something much broader: in Paris, desire was treated as a leavening agent that pitched disparate classes of people into an ungainly tangle of corporal delight. French men and women "horizontally collaborated" to overcome all social obstacles, divisions, and regulations. This included married and unmarried couples, straights and homosexuals, foreigners and locals, gun-toting soldiers and their vanquished subjects. The natural yearning for sexual pleasure, for the touch of another human body, equally corrupted the cohabiting partners. This was a shared wondrous descent that Parisians were said to have perfected. ✣

HORIZONTAL
COLLABORATION

"Girls, ze Americain Ambassador he is so wondaireful—
he says he wants ze peace at any price."

PARIS PLAISIRS

In Paris, the map of mankind's hidden passions is teasingly displayed. It is the one metropolis where all of the secret desires of the world can be gratified.

— Pierre Mac Orlan, *La Seine*, 1927 —

The Frenchman takes his sin in easy fashion and not just to be naughty. His depravity is often charming.

— Basil Woon, *The Paris That's Not in the Guide Books*, 1926 —

FEW HISTORIC OR CONTEMPORARY SITES have been more identified with hedonistic pursuits and sensual enchantment than Paris. For centuries, the French capital has been the erotic lodestone for lust-smitten ramblers. No regime changes, riots, violent revolutions, wars, or foreign invasions have sullied its exalted urban status. Jaded and love-wary nomads from every nation have sought out Paris' tawdry offerings and singular institutions of pleasure.

OPPOSITE: George Brassaï, *At Suzy's*, 1932

RIGHT: Braig, *A Memory of Paris*, 1938

It was here that sex, avant-garde art, popular music, epicurean dining, seasonal pageants of *au courant* fashion, social dance, mind-shattering intoxicants, romantic strolls, high literature, and variety entertainment forms melded into modern European culture. And it was in Paris that sin became "silkened," exposed, sanctified, and readily purchased.

For much of the city's thousand-year history, even beggars and the lower classes were encouraged to indulge in the carnal pastimes that were the purview of royalty and the moneyed elites elsewhere. Sexual arousal in all its countless mechanisms was not only a Parisian *métier* for international tourism; it reconfigured the psychology and lifestyles of its resident population and attracted a constant stream of freethinking immigrants and refugees. Their contributions substantially added to the metropolis' already shady allure. In Paris' Montmartre district alone, one could partake in the wildest antics of nocturnal Buenos Aires, *Alt-Wien*, Harlem, Imperial Russia, Barcelona, Heaven, Hell, or the putrefaction of the Grave — all within a stop or two of the Place Blanche Métro station.

Paris stimulated desire, paraded it in its streets and brothels, discussed it in its salons and journals, celebrated and laughed at it in its galleries, dance halls, nightclubs, and revue houses. The City of Light *(la Ville-Lumière)* was reputed to be Europe's Counter-Vatican. Even small-town constables, radical reactionaries and Fascist chieftains, clerics and social utopians, staid businessmen and their hapless wives fell victim to Paris' lurid charms. Few could resist its erotic pulse or outpace the sensory quicksand of Pigalle that engulfed all notions of moral rectitude or bourgeois restraint.

THE FIRST FRENCHMAN

Hundreds of academic studies — filling the open-air bookstalls on both sides on the Seine — have attempted to track down the precise origin of Gallic profligacy and its dramatic displays. Many pointed to the era of Charlemagne (768–814) or even centuries earlier, when Roman chroniclers marveled unabashedly at the lusty, if shockingly barbarian, Frankish folkways. During the 1920s and 1930s, however, one historical personality resurfaced on the music-hall stages as the inventor of modern French culture, single-handedly promoting the erotic glory of his people and their excessively randy court. This was François I (1494–1547), the warrior-king, whose love of Italian culture and slim-hipped women nearly bankrupted the monarchy by the end of his reign.

The Valois ruler created a national library, which he filled with rare books and ancient manuscripts, had his agents ship plaza-sized art works from Northern Italy to Paris, built or redesigned architectural palaces, including the Louvre, and employed Europe's best-known soothsayers and graphic artists, like Nostradamus and Leonardo da Vinci.

François was rumored to have enjoyed the services of a royal mistress at the tender age of ten before graduating into the incestuous embraces of his older sister. After he was crowned in 1515, the womanizing regent designated his courtesans and playthings with official titles and branded their backsides with the regal *fleur de lys*. (Once the floral symbol of Mary's purity, it soon acquired another meaning: an engorged phallus between two willing legs.) During the first half of the sixteenth century, the lily-of-the-field became the standard emblem of François' haughty regime.

ABOVE: Russell Patterson, *Arc de Triomphe*, 1935

BELOW LEFT: Chéri Hérouard, *A Demonic Consort*, 1927

BELOW RIGHT: Lucien Jaquelux, *The Blasphemous Court*, 1924

ABOVE: Folies Bergère, *The Folies of Folies: "The Royal Advisors,"* 1934

When not engaged in full-scale warfare or nefarious peacetime diplomacy, the *savoir-faire* monarch invented *haute cuisine*, promoted the fastidious art of witty dinner repartee, and championed the opulent presentations of slinky female *couture*, replete with all its plush accessories and sparkling-eyed, immobile models.

The king also befriended the literary mastermind François Rabelais (1483–1553), who, after being schooled in a monastery, turned to the secular arts. This crafty wordsmith wrote both ribald couplets about the debauched French court and the Renaissance's most irreverently scatological novels, *Pantagruel* and *Gargantua*. Although banned by the Sorbonne's pious and dutiful board of artistic decorum and decency, these pornographic fables found their way into France's upper echelons. They were read to the hard-partying sovereign and his entourage during their festive evening repasts.

When Emperor Joseph of Austro-Hungary came to Paris on a ceremonial visit in 1541, he was astonished to hear François proclaim Rouyon as his country's largest city. "What about Paris?" the Austrian noble politely inquired. The French ruler's playful retort, "Paris is a separate nation," exacted a stately chortle and later found its way into the municipality's fêted and impudent folklore.

According to official accounts, the fifty-two-year-old François died from an inflammation of the urinary bladder in 1547. Others believed the actual culprit was syphilis, a disease that France's chivalrous navigators had carried back from their rough-and-tumble exploits in the New World.

THE AUTHENTIC FAITH OF *LA BELLE FRANCE*

Religious wars riled the French countryside long before the Calvinist Awakening during François' regime. Yet the horrific accounts of the Reformation conflict — the appalling atrocities undertaken by enraged parishioners against rival congregants, destruction of church sanctuaries and holy relics, communal massacres, and public execution of ecclesiastical authorities — often ignore one important demographic feature: the majority of the French townspeople supported neither the tainted Catholic hierarchy and their supporters nor its morally rigid opposition, the crusadingly iconoclastic Protestant pastorate. For the most part, French laity gravitated toward an older belief system known as *plaisirs*, or pleasure.

Despite their provincial divisions and maddening allegiances to a wide spectrum of sectarian creeds, dialects, extended clans, occupations, and political faiths, the inhabitants of fractious Gaul were united by a devotion to their cornucopia of earthly indulgences. True, the nation had one seat of power and one recognized head of state but it also produced over four hundred varieties of cheese and an assortment of some ninety regionally distinct wines and alcoholic potions. France had tied its tribal identification and proclamation of national autonomy to the quest for sensory gratification. Two centuries before the iconic image of Marianne (flashing one perfectly shaped bare breast) became the universal emblem of the revolutionary Republic, political cartoonists drew captivating young women to symbolize the French monarchy and its pleasure-seeking polis.

BELOW: Folies Bergère, *A Folies' Smash: "The Cloister,"* 1930

ABOVE: Folies Bergère, *Women of the Follies: "Night of Casanova's Orgy,"* 1933

Sunday in pre-Revolutionary France may have been a sacred respite devoted to otherworldly endeavors, a mandated period for early morning prayer, solemn reflection, and spiritual as well as material sacrifice, but the rest of the week veered toward more corporal non-Christian diversions: drunken brawls, whoring, night-long banquets, wanton encounters, gambling, and rancorous entertainments.

To the dismay of the Vatican apparatchiks, even newly instituted church holidays, like the Feast of Corpus Christi that commemorated the Mystery of the Holy Eucharist, quickly jettisoned their somber theophoric rites and transformed into community free-for-alls, nonstop masquerades, and grotesquely comic processionals. During the late Renaissance, in France alone, the Corpus Christi observance grew exponentially in size from several days to whole months. Behind all of it was the unremitting thirst for sybaritic bliss.

And in no other country was anti-clericalism was so rampant and so laughably eroticized. When not depicted as congenital drunkards or gluttons, tonsure-shaved monks and priests were commonly satirized as flesh-mad miscreants. Every French minstrel possessed a thick trove of ballads and rhymed stories about obsessively virtuous clergymen and mother superiors who were perversely brought down by one particular kind of physical temptation: the noxious contagion of sexual ardor.

PORCELAIN BUTTOCKS ON THE GOLDEN THRONE

The delicious gossip that permeated France's imperial past was spectacularly re-enacted on the Parisian variety stages throughout the interwar era. Few notable avatars of public decency or supreme authority were spared the leering treatment of the music-hall impresarios and their prolific scribes. The tabloid mentality that transfixed the city's underclass was now employed to bemuse and unnerve Paris' educated elite. Antique episodes of illicit and clamorous misbehavior vaulted from subterranean invective into stageworthy divertissement.

At the Casino de Paris in 1927, François' inquisitive daughter-in-law, Catherine de Medici, peered through a partition in the floor of her palace bedroom to balefully observe her husband, Henri II, make impetuous love to his mistress. Reviewers crowed that the Casino's scandalized first-nighters mirrored Catherine's gap-jawed stance. In 1933, the Folies Bergère graphically portrayed Giacomo Casanova's toxic influence on the French court in Versailles with a celebrated nude sketch entitled "Night of Casanova's Orgy." (Ah, those decadent Venetians!)

The 1928 season of the Moulin Rouge featured a controversial number about Madame du Barry's foot-fetish seduction of Louis XV, which concluded with her trial at a Revolutionary tribunal and subsequent beheading. Moreover, all five of Paris' leading music-hall emporiums routinely parodied Napoleon's addled infatuation with the sexually unquenchable Joséphine and the erotic excesses of his namesake's Second Empire.

For revue-going Parisians of the 1920s and 1930s, national reverence for the pantheon of Gaul's legendary icons was comically upended with arresting theatrical images of foppish cowards in oversized epaulets and military regalia, vain bare-breasted courtesans, diplomatic double-talkers, and duplicitous aristocrats plotting outrageous trysts. French popular culture had altered the Academy's master narrative. To the average spectator in Jazz-Age Paris, costumed historical figures were no less unsavory than the ubiquitous Panama-hatted *boulevardiers*, who sniffed out the latest neighborhood thrill.

IN THE REALM OF THE ENLIGHTENMENT AND ROYAL IMPIETY

During the American Revolution, according to Benjamin Franklin, the "City of Silken Sin" had already accommodated itself to two hundred years of sex tourism and, since 1655, produced wagonloads of handcrafted erotic artifacts and pornographic booklets for travel-weary shut-ins. In fact, the 14,000 registered prostitutes that strutted down Paris' winding thoroughfares or haunted the foyers of its hotels and taverns would, during the first years of the rebellion, outnumber George Washington's puny Colonial army. To the warring citizens of both Philadelphia and London, Paris was synonymous with readily available and government-regulated sex.

Among Louis XVI's besotted gentry and their phalanx of powdered courtiers, up-to-date eroticism intertwined with medical science and occult fashion. In 1778,

the Swabian physician, alchemist, and mellifluous confidence man, Franz Anton Mesmer (1734–1815), introduced animal magnetism, hypnotic induction, and mechanical cures that utilized pulsating electrical charges to patrician French audiences. Every arousal disorder, including impotence and frigidity, could be treated with a suggestive sweep of the hand, evocative command, or spark from a mysterious battery coil.

According to Mesmerian doctrine, invisible magnetic rays or "fluids" streamed across the universe, animating matter and enhancing anatomic vitality. In fact, Mesmer

and his disciples proclaimed that the human body itself was a soft-tissue magnet with "receptor poles" and discernible fields of energy. Illness, physical incapacity, ennui, or congenital disease was merely a manifestation of "terrestrial fluid blockage." These harmonious imbalances could be corrected during all-night séances, where individual

patients were initiated into somnambulist trance-states, seated knee-to-knee before the stone-faced master who held their hands and made slow passes across their bodies, or had the sides of their breasts vigorously massaged.

As his aristocratic clientele rapidly expanded, Mesmer constructed a novel means to generate magnetic flow for groups of twenty or more. Giggling "chains" of devotees were bound to large tubs of galvanized iron filings in water, called *baquets*. Affixed to these wooden contraptions were twisted metal bars that radiated healing beams.

Mesmer's sometimes hysteria-inducing ceremonies concluded with soothing and restorative music, played on a glass harmonium.

To its many adversaries — and even to some of its followers — the cult of Mesmer trafficked in sensationalist, hyper-dramatic, orgiastic showmanship reconfigured as therapeutic public health. The vast majority of the goodly doctor's compliant subjects were said to be conjugally neglected housewives from Paris' privileged classes and upper crust. Mesmerism, in the end, was the ultimate act of scientific chicanery in the service of Enlightenment philosophy and facile psychological seduction.

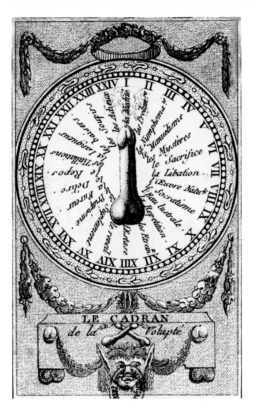 

LEFT: *The Dial of Voluptuous Pleasure*, c. 1775

RIGHT: Félix Nogaret, *The French Aretino*, 1787

FRATERNITÉ PORNOGRAPHERS

Official censorship of French publications, once the excusive domain of the Church, passed into government hands in 1629. As the methods of printing advanced and literacy became more widespread, ideological threats to the social order proliferated through the seventeenth and eighteenth centuries. The Monarchy attempted to control and suppress them at all costs. Mass-market books that endorsed agnosticism, libertine or freethinking beliefs, seditious sentiments, or controversial political treatises were scrupulously banned. And the imperial punishments for the wayward publishers and booksellers turned shockingly draconian — anywhere from permanent banishment to incarceration to public execution.

Erotica and insurgent protest literature had gone underground, but only marginally, chiefly because the demand for it could not be easily stifled. Feisty Parisians could surreptitiously purchase "immoral" pamphlets on the cheap in the galleries of Palais Royal, where licensed prostitutes hawked their services. The lure of the forbidden naturally enhanced sales and churned out a new crop of buccaneering authors.

In fact, the enterprising countercultural theologians perfected a new genre: clandestine radical tracts laced with copious reports of blasphemous sexuality. For the most part, they were mock scandal sheets with detailed accounts of highborn perversions, ribald exploits of the wardens of earthly virtue, and their incredulous self-justifications for depraved behavior.

These fiendish anti-establishment/pornographic concoctions were ironically known in the trade as *livres philosophiques* ("philosophical books"). Their actual descriptive style, however, was accorded a less delicate rubric: *foutromanie*, or "fuck-mania." The readership of these tarted-up brochures traversed all class divisions and they gave a satirical voice to the unstable political climate.

LEFT: *The Uterine Furies of Marie Antoinette*, 1791

BELOW: Marquis de Sade, *The Story of Juliette, or the Rewards of Vice*, 1797

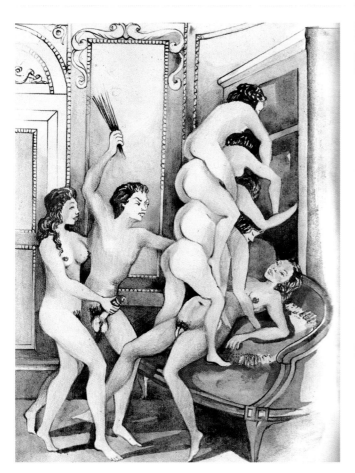

ABOVE: Marquis de Sade, *The New Justine, or the Misfortunes of Virtue*, 1797

Two writers emerged from the pool of dissident French pornographers, Marquis de Sade (1740–1814) and Restif de la Bretonne (1734–1806). Bitter enemies, their unsavory reputations outlived the Ages of Reason and Revolution. And each reaped considerably more literary accolades and praise for their intellectual gravitas in the twentieth century than during their own lifetimes. Together they penned over five hundred novels, plays, anti-Monarchist manifestos, and autobiographical *romans à clef,* most of which were lost in revolutionary conflagration or officially pulped by the ubiquitous republican Committees of Public Safety.

Born into one of France's oldest noble families, Donatien Alphonse François de Sade pursued a military career during the Seven Years War, attaining the formal rank of captain. Shortly after his retirement from the Royal Dragoon Regiment in 1763, de Sade was accused of brutal mistreatment by a trio of prostitutes, whom he procured off the streets of Paris. The arraignment involved charges of physical assault — acute flagellation and lacerations with a knife. It was the first of many such proceedings against the young reprobate.

During this time, the Marquis built a private theatre in his nearby *château* and, later, a more elaborate one at his family estate in the South. There, his love for violent fantasy, nihilistic philosophy, pornographic *tableaux vivants*, and fanatical anti-clericalism merged. Malevolent infantile caprice polluted his thoughts and animated his monstrous conduct. In his subversive and debauched imagination, coitus and cruelty had become interchangeable.

According to de Sade's torrent of antinomian proclamations, every arm or theory of moral regulation had to be viciously and relentlessly confronted. In court and before government censors, the despotic aristocrat demanded absolute erotic freedom. Humanity's erogenous zones could not be delimited to a few sensitive regions. Punitive whippings, gender-blind sodomy, base humiliation and excruciating torture, ritual masturbation, deflowering of children, bestiality, the penetration of all of the body's orifices, these were the Marquis' scenarios that extolled unadulterated carnal rapture. And only the most exquisite and harrowing dreamscapes made flesh could lead to genuine spiritual liberation.

The irate American feminists of the 1970s and the solipsistic French pornographer shared one common belief: all sex was rape — usually camouflaged in various cloaks of social propriety.

The high-collared bureaucrats from Louis', Robespierre's, and Napoleon's administrations, however, rendered a different judgment: de Sade and his iniquitous ideas had to be excised from the community at large. In fact, the "divine marquis" was sentenced to thirty-two of his remaining forty-six years to confinement in prison, much of it in solitary detention, or to lunatic asylums. Napoleon himself denounced de Sade as a supreme menace to the tranquility of his Empire. The term *sadisme* soon entered the nineteenth-century vocabulary of French jurisprudence and psychopathology. It was defined as the psychic rush that a sexual deviant experiences after the infliction of pain.

BELOW: Restif de la Bretonne, *Anti-Justine, or the Delights of Love,* 1798

Although de Sade's extant fiction has been respectfully probed and lionized by modernist French critics, beginning with the Surrealists, the Marquis' contemporaries found his *oeuvre* excessively repetitive, long-winded, illusory, and, to be sure, emotionally tedious. If the obvious goal of pornography was mental titillation, then de Sade's scabrous narratives failed. Even Paris' vigilant vice police ignored them.

What ensured the books' historical notoriety, however, were the illustrations that were appended to the 1797 editions. Here, anonymous artists gave a baroque and art-brutish shape to the dissolute philosopher's impossible and frightening copulatory revelations. Sadly, the names of the faithful decoders of de Sade's deranged apparitions have been lost to history.

Nicolas-Edme Restif de la Bretonne returned pornography to its smutty naturalistic roots. An incest-haunted roué and voyeur of nighttime Paris, he

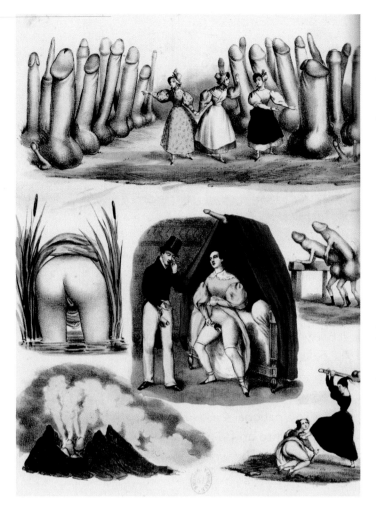

ABOVE: *Pastimes* Lithograph, 1840

mined his own untidy life for tales of amorality and promiscuous adventure. The father of over twenty illegitimate offspring and lover of hundreds of dainty-shoed Parisiennes, Restif dutifully catalogued his conquests in diary-like novels. Sometimes he listed the strumpets' personal histories, lewd activities, splendid physical façades, and the calendar of his seductions, but usually he lingered on their feet and laced boots.

Restif was a foot fetishist *par excellence*. He marveled at the velvety textures, beckoning shapes, locomotion, subjugating pheromones, and piquant smells of the naked female foot and its silken and leather-bound wraps. After recklessly impregnating two of his daughters, the rake claimed that his greatest fear was blindly caressing and worshipping the limbs of one of his out-of-wedlock brood. That is why he routinely interrogated the city's streetwalkers before lifting their dresses and smothering their pungent soles with appreciative kisses.

Like de Sade, whom he denounced as one of three living ogres — the others being his ex-wife and son-in-law — the self-described "Owl of Paris" was an early and enthusiastic supporter of the Revolution. As an unconventional social reformer, Restif endured censorship and destitution during the Region of Terror. The visionary philanderer had presciently called for the formation of state-run brothels, universal medical care, a five-day workweek, and the United States of Europe.

THE NEW CENTURY

Much of Paris' modern sex culture crystallized during the Napoleonic era and in the sobering decades of the Bourbon Restoration that followed. Provocative displays of full-frontal nudity, indecent political exposés, and angry hardcore erotica softened and were reconfigured into coy, more lighthearted, and teasing renditions. The former bare-breasted Amazons of Revolution now were likely to be cloaked in diaphanous gowns with flasks of water affixed to their elongating, above-the-stomach sashes. The perfumed water was splashed across their upper torsos, producing a wet-T-shirt look.

The divorce laws, initiated in the early years of the Revolution, continued under the Napoleonic Code but priestly marriage did not. (Not only did many radical clerics renounce their vows of chastity in 1793, they insisted on wedding extremely comely maidens in order to demonstrate their allegiance as worthy *citoyens* to the New France.)

Intergenerational seduction, adultery, "free marriage," and adult flirtation grew into a distinct art form and commanded a new etiquette and sense of gamesmanship (*esprit de la vie*). Despite a divergent set of rules and consequences for the genders, Parisiennes felt newly enfranchised. Feminine and masculine desires had elegantly convened on the dance floor with an arsenal of competing steps and strategies. *Vive la différence!*

As the population of Paris doubled and then tripled between 1800 and 1860, urban renewal and new technologies multiplied the metropolis' erotic possibilities. Its intricate sexual tapestry broadened and thrived with the Industrial Revolution's advance. More than Manchester or Dresden, the French Gotham was lauded as the hub of secular/progressive Western civilization. Thanks to a national railroad system that crisscrossed the entire countryside, Paris swelled into an Eden of strangers, a paradise of anonymous social contact. Here, married men and women could live like bachelors or free-spirited coquettes; and bachelors and single women as pashas or feckless dowagers.

In the course of Napoleon III's Second Empire, the physical character of *la ville de Paris* underwent a major transformation. Baron Haussmann redesigned the antediluvian cityscape, wrecking cobblestone pathways and neighborhoods in order to seamlessly connect, aggrandize, and fuse its autonomous districts. Civic planners unwittingly thrust the packs of furtive streetwalkers into its unbounded Grands Boulevards. Paris became known in equal measures as a citadel of international exchange, immense bourgeois luxury, artistic sophistication, industrial innovation, and sex trafficking, as well as a dumping ground for French peasants turned laborer or shopkeeper. Although the outlying proletarian *arrondissements* (*la Zone*) were unspeakable eyesores, they contained the ideal human reservoir for Paris' colossal urban expansion.

ABOVE AND BELOW: Erotic Phénakistiscope Disk, c. 1835

BELOW: *Reclining Nude* Daguerreotype, c. 1850; *Nude Wearing a Veil* Stereoscopic Daguerreotype, c. 1850

In 1841, two years after the invention of the daguerreotype in Paris, a lucrative subgenre began to surface in the side streets of Montmartre: photographic pornography. These printed images of naked models in fetishist poses and often-comic couplings were cheap to fabricate, relatively easy to sell, and had devoted collectors, who could casually hide their chemically-treated glass-plate or paper purchases inside stacks of touristy postcards and pamphlets. London and New York had covert emporiums of modern erotica, but in Paris, enterprising merchants created a veritable cottage industry. French photographers and dealers mass-produced their illicit *objets d'art* and peddled them wherever foreigners thronged.

Before the collapse of the Empire in 1870, street constables repeatedly arrested the "vendors of immorality" (in their telltale loose-fitting raincoats that concealed the forbidden goods) outside theatre doorways and train stations. Vice inspectors raided and shuttered scores of unauthorized film studios in Pigalle, confiscating tens of thousands of obscene engravings and negatives. Aggravated magistrates sentenced the petty pornographers and their brazen subjects to lengthy prison terms (average incarceration for female nudes, fifty-one days; male nudes, 168 days).

Yet the licentious commerce flourished. It was the latest — and highly marketable — attraction of *la Ville-Lumière*. "Filthy" French postcards would be hawked throughout the world and endure as a derisory cultural artifact for the better part of a century.

RIGHT: Erotic Postcard, c. 1890

LA BELLE ÉPOQUE

By the 1880s, the portrait of *Paris mondain* as an erotic wonderland was securely fixed in the imaginations of European and transatlantic sightseers. Entertainment venues, especially tiny cabarets and literary cafés, once the private salons for avant-garde authors, graphic artists, journalists, and performers, overnight attracted affluent locals and in-the-know tourists. The bohemian "Spirit of Montmartre" engendered an aesthetic underground of both experimental art and unfettered social mores. Outsiders could marvel at the hothouse environment of goateed painters in their splattered smocks, anarchist poets, and smug *conférenciers* within arms' reach of the shameless nudes and all the other saucy inspirations of the said *artistes*.

The best known of these rakish Montmartre emporiums was the Chat Noir — equal parts wild-boy tavern, cramped music-hall, and informal haven for pipe-smoking reporters and amateur *chansonniers*. It was Paris' first cabaret. A mock Swiss sentry stood guard at its doorway, impeding any efforts by bourgeois curiosity-seekers to check out its eccentric attractions, which included the adolescent "skull" of Louis VIII. When it opened in 1881, the disreputable Left Bank club of poets and painters, *Les Hydropathes* ("The Water Dreaders") made the Chat their permanent home for swilling cheap wine and beer. Here was an ideal venue for comic recitation, hurdy-gurdy street ballads, and assorted anti-establishment raunch.

After a move to a larger venue three years later, the Chat Noir featured an adult shadow puppet show and had its own (identically named) avant-garde journal, which was sold in nearby kiosks. One common dirty refrain on the street was the question to ragamuffin newspaper vendors, "Madame, do you have *Le Chat Noir* ['a black pussy']?" Within a decade, even soused packs of bankers were annoying female peddlers on the Boulevard de Clichy with that enduringly witless query.

During the next twenty years, a dozen more intimate nightspots and artistic cafés put out welcoming mats near the Place Pigalle for its colorful habitués and their growing clientele. Streetwalkers, absinthe-addicted clerks, hirsute intellectuals, fast-draw caricaturists, gold-toothed *Alphonses*, cancan dancers from the nearby music-halls, and bowler-hatted poets finally had a fashionable destination to while away their evenings and meager earnings.

Impressionist painters covered the cabaret walls and window frames with their gaudy canvases and eye-catching prints. And as the theatrical entertainments became more accomplished and equally more sordid, rowdy tourists followed in their wake. Crimson-haired *filles de joie* competed with the slinky performers for the erotic attention of bedazzled spectators.

Toulouse-Lautrec was not the only Frenchman who perceived the 9th and 18th

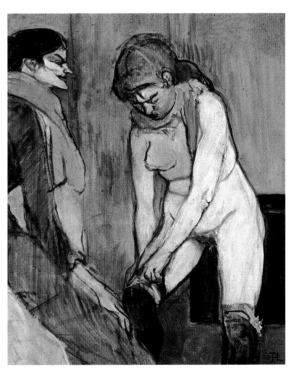

TOP: Jean de Paleologu, *The Mad Cow Procession* Poster, 1896

BOTTOM: Henri de Toulouse-Lautrec, *Woman Pulling Up a Stocking*, 1894

arrondissements as a voyeur's wet dream, an urban stockade, or barnyard, of leggy female flesh diaphanously demarcated in black lace.

In the midst of *La Belle Époque,* tens of thousands of teenagers and single women from the countryside deserted their familial surroundings and were promptly sucked into the maw of France's insatiable industrial centers. Most eked out livings on dank factory floors or in bourgeois households but some struck out for more raffish milieus.

The Symbolist poet, Jean Moréas succinctly captured the public fascination with Montmartre's increasingly louche ambiance in his 1886 novel, *Le Thé Chez Miranda*: "All those pretty girls landed up on the streets of Paris with breasts too large for their slight scruples."

THE TWENTIETH CENTURY

By the time Gustave Eiffel's iron lattice Tower was erected in 1899, the infectious Pigalle-ism had spread across the city. Substantial numbers of genteel Parisians now fancied themselves as contemporary "flowers of evil." Charles Baudelaire and the Decadent poets were no longer outré debauchees of a moldering conurbation but clairvoyant visionaries of a new era.

Many French journalists hailed the cultural upheaval that they observed everywhere in the city. Lighthearted flirtation had become the most commonplace means of social interaction. By the newest definition, a Parisienne was a pouty-faced vixen or *bien soignée* creature, who knew how to punctuate a conversation with the occasional smoothing of her blouse, giddy sigh, sustained touching, cursory side-glances, and a knowing carmined smile. A shimmering web of Eros had enveloped the entire metropolis. The phallic-shaped silhouette of the Eiffel Tower at night signaled European *bons vivants* that a modern Tower of Babel awaited them.

At the turn of the century, "Parisian sexuality" conjured up a voyeuristic panorama of universal lust — scandalous visions where both female and male paramours nonchalantly divulged their feral affections. In the minds of prurient bystanders, "French kissing" obliged a reciprocated flamboyancy: the interplay of tongues between two receptive mouths. For the city's *flâneurs*, this was practically a public display of fellatio or cunnilingus. Even wedded Parisiennes flaunted their pretty stems in indecent silk-stockinged repose — not only in the boudoir but also in the showroom and on the street. After all, these urbane women were the first to be liberated and freed from the antiquated morality of the nineteenth century's double standards.

Parisian men were also viewed as a new species of mankind. They tolerated their partners' wandering attentions and open promiscuity without a sense of

TOP: Victor Meuzy, *Guide for the Stranger in Montmartre*, 1900

BOTTOM: Xavier Sager, *Montmartre* Postcard, 1900

OPPOSITE: Images from Pathé advertisement

jealousy or possessiveness. A kind of Descartian logic applied to human desire in Paris. Any Champagne dinner assumed erotic participation, preceded by a stratagem of mutual foreplay. What mattered most to onlookers was the physical attractiveness of the couples or the internal French construction known as "sex-appeal."

The latest technologies also confirmed the iniquitous repute of *fin-de-siècle* Paris. Explicit motion pictures appeared just a few months after the Lumière brothers' invention stupefied traditional music-hall audiences. The coarse Pathé shorts, however, were expensive to make, extremely bulky to cart around, required special equipment to project, and could only be shown in the most secretive of venues.

PREWAR PARISIAN SEXUAL SLANG
(Parigot)

BRANLETTE ("Sword Play"): Manual sex, masturbation. [Also a term for "masturbator" or "worthless."]

BRANLETTE ESPAGNOLE ("Spanish Masturbation"): Genital frottage between the breasts, or a tit job.

CACHE-CACHE ("Hide and Seek"): To make love.

EPICIÈRE ("Spice up"): Normal intercourse.

FAIRE L'ABATTAGE ("Making the Slaughter"): To fuck a whore.

FAIRE LA PETITE CHAPELLE ("Making the Little Chapel"): When a woman exposed her breasts (or provocatively primped her blouse).

FAIRE LE TRUC/LA RETAPE ("Making the Trick/the Fix"): What a hooker did on the street.

FAIRE MINETTE ("Making the Cat"): Cunnilingus, muff diving.

MÉTHODE ANGLAISE ("English Method"): Tied to a cross and whipped.

PATTES D'ARAIGNÉE ("Spider Legs"): To manually excite.

PUCES TRAVAILLEUSES ("Flea work"): Lesbian sex play.

SOIXANTE-NEUF ("69"): Mutual oral sex. French specialty.

SPÉ: An erotic forte.

TAILLER UNE PIPE ("Cutting a Tube"): Fellatio.

TAILLER UNE PLUME ("Slashing with a Feather"): Erotic whipping.

GRANDE CONSTRUCTION

Until the late 1920s, erotic films made in France had very limited outlets: "gentlemen's tents" in traveling carnivals, luxury brothels, private projection houses, and after-hours men's clubs. These smokers, as they were soon labeled because of the tobacco fumes that filled their darkened halls, were basically flesh-bearing stills that showcased weird and perverse sexual activities. They were primitive in terms of character, scenic design, plot, and cinematography. Credits, when they were included, were brief and jokey. Neither the performers nor the filmmakers could be considered artists or highly skilled purveyors of the new medium. As a marketable enterprise, French pornographic cinema had a tiny, if enthusiastic, audience and a droll underground reputation.

In another way, the sexual awakening of France's emergent middle class before World War I could be calculated by the enormous increase in municipal brothels. These were authorized and policed by appointed commissioners. They grew in number from a mere handful in 1890 to over four hundred by 1914. Paris alone had 221 legal *maisons closes*.

The illustrated humor monthly *Le Rire* underscored their popularity and social hypocrisy in 1904 with a two-page layout entitled "The Secret Boîte of Nevers." Designed as a put-together children's dollhouse with separate standalone figures, it detailed all the inner workings of a three-storied bordello. Among the clients was the city's mayor, wrapped in a tricolored sash. Following him up the stairs were the town notables, which could be cranked up to the first-floor parlor in a single line. Inside the salon, a dozen prostitutes received them with perky nude salutations. The seated brothel owners appeared to be reading newspapers and were completely distracted from the ceremonial frenzy.

OPPOSITE: *La Boîte secrète de Nevers* (*Le Rire* #78, July 30, 1904)

BELOW: George Scott, *For the Flag! For the Victory!* 1917

THE WAR CALLED GREAT

The onset of World War I spawned one unforeseen social dilemma for the belligerent nations. The general conscription of able-bodied men in Europe meant that the status of women in the workforce had to be reconsidered. Each country needed a vast assortment of rearguard laborers and civil servants. This was a boon to the suffrage movement but created incalculable havoc for the interior ministers and their bureaucratic underlings. Women of all ages were supposed to be the inspirational icons for each state's valiant servicemen, not their behind-the-scenes replacements. This imperiled the notion of traditional patriotic morale.

In France, the role and support of female noncombatants, although a necessary imperative, rattled the civic order. The defeat of the French armies in the Franco-Prussian War in 1870 called into question the readiness and ability of the military to adequately defend the homeland. While tabloid banners on every kiosk alerted passersby to the Kaiser's aggressive ambitions, one *sotto voce* topic in the cafés bordered on the subversive: were

SOUSCRIVEZ à L'EMPRUNT NATIONAL
LES SOUSCRIPTIONS SONT REÇUES A PARIS ET EN PROVINCE
À LA
BANQUE NATIONALE DE CRÉDIT

PARIS PENDANT LA GUERR

Frenchmen sufficiently assertive to ensure the safety of the Republic? Of course, French women from every social strata could do their part as field hands, unpaid nurses, day laborers in armament plants, and temporary administrators but they had to maintain their femininity and *joie de vivre* outlook while doing so.

In 1915, six months after the savage fighting had stalemated into trench warfare, a peculiar French institution was launched, *marraines de guerre* ("wartime godmothers"). This was a voluntary service that bonded patriotic Frenchwomen with "orphaned" or single men at the front. Bereft of domestic or female contacts, it was feared that the neglected French infantrymen, commonly branded as *poilus* (or "shaggies"), would soon fall into a stagnant, disabling malaise or become victims of the recently diagnosed condition known as shell shock.

The *marraines'* letters to their adopted sons (*filleuls*) were supposed to raise the boys' fighting spirits and reconcile them to the excruciating tedium, physical anguish, or still worse results of mechanized combat. The women's patronage was often reinforced through personally intimate language and erotic appeal (*la correspondance galante*). Both the *marraines* and the *poilus* promised to offer up their bodies for the preservation of the battered Third Republic.

Although the subject of endless journalistic parody, the *marraine* phenomenon did prove to be an effective wartime propaganda tool and another example of French exceptionalism in all matters related to sex. (Controlled prostitution in the urban centers actually declined because so many young whores had opted to

Les Marraines et les Filleuls au Pavillon Bleu, St Cloud

work in munitions' factories.) Upright bourgeois women now were the principal sources of soldierly relief and national recovery. No other warring state promoted anything like it.

One erotic interchange, however, proved to be unsettling for both the home-front heroes and the Central Powers' publicists. This was the attraction of Parisiennes, both the promiscuous and stay-at-home types, toward the multitude of Allied soldiers on leave and the 300,000 dark-skinned French troops from the Empire's African colonies. Fear of racial pollution and miscegenation created a panic that would outlast the Armistice and haunt German monarchists and reactionaries for decades.

In postwar Paris, however, interest in African-American culture and the public intermingling that resulted from it was another mark of the city's free-spirited morality and widening international sophistication.

PANAME DURING THE CRAZY YEARS

Among the Entente Powers, except for Czarist Russia, France suffered the greatest number of military and civilian casualties, nearly 1,700,000 deaths, over 4% of its total population. Yet, unlike the vanquished Berlin, Vienna and Budapest, Paris quickly revived. Newsreels of the continental Peace Conferences highlighted a delirious and glittering metropolis. Many Allied soldiers from deactivated units, waiting for their

ABOVE LEFT: Henri Gerbault, *He Remembers His Furlough*, 1916

ABOVE TOP: A hotel-restaurant in Saint-Cloud advertises its services, 1917

ABOVE BOTTOM: Chéri Hérouard, *First Night in the Marraine's Flat*, 1917

discharge papers, scouted out its furtive charms, which often produced a deeper impression and better talking points than any of their battlefield exploits.

Paris, universally referred to as *Paname* by the locals because of *de rigueur* hats worn by male fashion plates, was back in business. By 1923, over 250,000 American tourists had made their way across the Atlantic to explore the French capital. Fleeing their country's draconian Prohibition laws and flush with wads of hard currency, the worldly trekkers weren't just there to inspect the landmarks and museums or ferret out its fine dining establishments. They were drawn to *la Ville-Lumière* for a more unconventional list of enticements, many of which were primly catalogued in the city's official directories or featured in the voyagers' naughty guidebooks. ⚜

"Cocottes, Garçonnes, and Poules"

PARIS IS A WOMAN

In Paris strange womankind invites your smile and pouts when you do not yield.

— **Basil Woon, *The Paris That's Not in the Guide Books*, 1926** —

The Parisienne is an exceptional creature. She would be utterly inconceivable in a different atmosphere, outside the air of the capital. She is the most perfect creation produced in Paris.

— **Pierre La Mazière, *Paris — City of Glory*, 1931** —

CHAPTER 2

NOTHING MORE BEFUDDLED first-time tourists and travel writers than the countenance and attitude of ordinary Parisiennes. The unescorted ladies that they saw in the railroad stations and hotel lobbies, in the shops and cafés, on the boulevards and side streets, all seemed hyper-erotized. These feisty maidens radiated a peculiar *savoir faire*-like confidence and a smirking tolerance of lecherous male gaze. Even the youngest and the most matronly knew how to captivate with their upturned lips, provocative smiles, rouged faces, insolent postures, and conspicuous fashion sense. To outsiders, the entire female species in this urban paradise looked and acted like they were eminently fuckable.

OPPOSITE: Peter Weller, *The Apache Girl*, 1929

TOP LEFT: Atelier Elite, *Two Sous For Your Thoughts, Chéri*, 1931

TOP RIGHT: Jeanne Mammen, *The Student*, 1925

BELOW: Léon Bonnotte, *The Perfect Woman*, 1925

Consider the plight of the wide-eyed newcomers: only the most experienced or informed could readily ferret out the bourgeois teases from their more commercially available sisters. It was a source of constant embarrassment and local amusement.

The British journalist — and later Vichy collaborationist — Sisley Huddleston blamed the city's males for this confusion of roles: "Husbands expect their wives to possess the sophisticated charm, in toilette, appearance, speech, gestures, of — the French word must be used here — *poules*. Modesty has disappeared." (*Paris Salons, Cafés, Studios,* 1928)

FRENCH FLIRT

Long before the emancipation of middle-class women and the flapper revolution in postwar Anglo-Saxon society, Parisian *femmes* had established a novel archetype, the stylish and capricious French Flirt. Her characteristics were unmistakable: she was feckless and seductive in her everyday relationships; her revealing attire demanded attention; when not nightclubbing, she spent much of her time ensconced in her perfumed boudoir, primping and beauty-resting; her favored pastimes were casual encounters and the steps leading up to it. The French Flirt had no more abiding interest in child-rearing than a pre-Empire countess or nineteenth-century courtesan. Whether descended from royalty, a petty bourgeois family, salaried employees, or a simple prole from the provinces, she exuded independence and sexual agency. The arbitrators of modernism warmly welcomed her.

This Eve needed no apple to corrupt her Adams.

Popular interest in the French Flirt and her disconcerting traits peaked during the *fin-de-siècle* era. For muck-raking novelists and intellectuals, this vampiress

incarnation was intractably linked to urbanism, the inscrutability of female lust, mass culture, gender miscommunication, male sexual anxiety, suffrage proselytizing, colonial guilt, the revival of Black Masses, and Symbolist art. In other words, everything futuristic and socially disruptive.

The French decadent, Joris-Karl Huysmans, described the flirtatious Parisian vamp best in his much-read Satanist masterpiece, *Down Under*, published in 1891: "No longer was she merely the dancing-girl who extorts a cry of lust" but "a monstrous Beast of the Apocalypse, indifferent, irresponsible, insensible, poisoning."

ABOVE LEFT: Sergy, *The Devil's Accomplice*, 1922

ABOVE RIGHT: Étienne Le Rallic, *Suffering in Silence*, 1927

LA GARÇONNE

After the Great War, several types of the New Woman were inelegantly redefined in French men's magazines. Some were saddled with names formerly associated with streetwalkers, like *cocottes, gigolettes,* and *minettes*; other labels borrowed from the lexicon of the Paris music-hall — *figurantes, mannequins*, and *nues*. One appellation, however, garnered worldwide notoriety: *garçonnes.* It was the signature invention of Victor Margueritte (1866–1942), a minor, if respected, avant-garde playwright.

Margueritte's 1922 novel *La Garçonne* (and its companion volume that was released seven years later) sold over one million copies and was a Jazz-Age *success de scandale*. It launched a *moderne* and enduring category of counter-femininity:

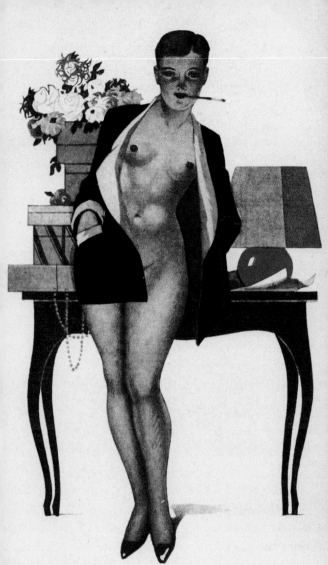

the eponymous Parisian "bachelorette." Within one year, it was translated into eight European languages.

The storybook heroine, Monique Lerbier, discovered the unfaithfulness of her caddish fiancé and escaped to Paris. There, a den of sophisticated lovers and debonair enablers sweet-talked her into their bedrooms and salons. A self-proclaimed tomboy, Monique hurriedly partook in the *au courant* thrills of cross-dressing, public carousing, workplace communalism, lesbian sex, and opium binges.

Just a few months after paperback copies of Margueritte's fiction hit the untidy counters of neighborhood kiosks, the term *garçonne* entered the daily patois and overnight replaced "flapper" in the French press. A 78 gramophone with the same title decisively secured its place in Parisian popular culture. (Previously, the little-used term delineated an elite class of butchy lesbians who paraded around in high hats and men's topcoats.)

Even the French film industry heeded *La Garçonne's* clarion call for female liberation. Luckily for the studio heads, the lurid pulp had folded the most traditional elements of melodrama into a contemporary urban setting. In 1923, a silent adaptation of Monique's travails and hedonistic forays was rushed into production and promptly banned by the civic authorities. The motion-picture censors had less success when it resurfaced in an overwrought 1936 sound version, featuring the scene-stealing *femmes du monde* Arletty and Édith Piaf. French moviegoers flocked to witness this curious spectacle of new womankind.

Margueritte's growing international reputation and immense earnings predictably sullied his official literary status. The provocateur's Legion of Honor designation was revoked in 1923. Margueritte did not even bother to dispute the charges of moral depravity. His racy narrative had broadened the path for anti-puritanical and free-spirited feminism.

FEMALE SUFFRAGE, SEX-APPEAL, AND THE NEW WOMAN

The women's suffrage movement gained traction in the United States and much of Europe during and immediately following World War I. In enlightened France, however, it suffered numerous setbacks. The National Assembly in 1922 chauvinistically rejected the enfranchisement of any citizens of the fairer sex. Shockingly, the most dismissive were the left-wing Deputies, who claimed that female voters would naturally support the Church and its reactionary partners. As mothers and anchors of familial stability, they were denounced as biologically conservative and opponents of the growing progressive current.

Frenchwomen were not granted the right to participate in any aspect of the electoral process until April 1944. (Even their names were dropped from municipal ballots.) That was when the Jesuit-trained General Charles de Gaulle, Commander of the Free French Forces, issued the grand proclamation of universal suffrage from his London headquarters. This was months before the Allied invasion and widely ignored. Eisenhower's attachés considered it one more inane Gaullist diversion.

LEFT: Georges Pavis, *Always So Feminine*, 1928

RIGHT: Julien Jacques Leclerc, *The Future Mode in National Elections*, 1925

LEFT: Léon Bonnotte, *Eugenics*, 1925

RIGHT: *Paris Sex-Appeal* (October 1935)

OPPOSITE TOP LEFT: *Paris Plaisirs* (November 1932)

OPPOSITE TOP RIGHT: Pem, *The Experts from Le Sourire Search for the Perfect Eve*, 1933

OPPOSITE BOTTOM: Granére Székács, *Bread From the Oven*, 1935

For the most part, Parisian women, during the interwar years, shrugged off their deflated legal status. They and the flowering expatriate community of like-minded females had discovered new freedoms in the laissez-faire capital. Labor shortages and a breezy permissive attitude had its rewards — financial and moral independence.

Shopgirls could live and work in big-city isolation, unobserved by town gossips or disapproving relatives. Their private recreations, like reading and filmgoing, still depicted sentimental romance but now the stories percolated with an infusion of sexual possibility. Many self-reliant ladies in the smart set — especially well-heeled lesbians — formed their own avant-garde identities. Women's bookstores, galleries, poetry presses, and salons sprung up in Montparnasse and beyond.

Sex-Appeal was another matter and a growing obsession among Parisians. During the decades when Frenchwomen were rebuffed in the political sphere, their erotic capital markedly escalated. Images of self-assured and unabashed *femmes* were paraded everywhere — in the revue houses, on the cinema screens, and, most tellingly, in the girly magazines that proliferated throughout the 1920s and 1930s.

Soignées Parisiennes possessed some dazzling trump cards. As the newfangled rogue gender, they had the capacity to ridicule their impotent and crestfallen soulmates; to humiliate through cuckoldry; and to shame with public exposure. Even the nudes in their colorful tranquility flashed tempestuous sneers. It was an alternative *ludus novus* that defined the city's topsy-turvy social relations and sex-crazed milieu.

Male Parisians responded with a malicious counter-sport. Women's physiques, their giddy choice of personal constructs, and intimate body parts could be measured and "scientifically" evaluated. This rationalization of female flesh was, to be sure, a comic enterprise. But beneath its playful treatment lurked a subversive coda: raw Sex-Appeal had a purely commercial and mechanical basis. Erotic attraction could be purchased in specialty emporiums, metrically calculated, and subjected to exacting industrial standards.

Malina Dorsowna
Bergères

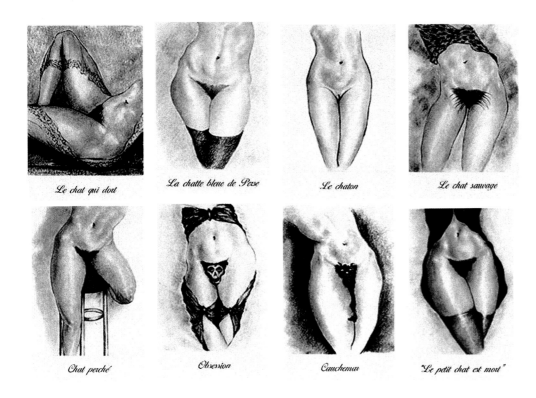

Le chat qui dort | La chatte bleue de Perse | Le chaton | Le chat sauvage

Chat perché | Obsession | Cauchemar | "Le petit chat est mort"

OPPOSITE: Folies Bergère, *The Folies' Factory: "Minting Women,"* 1931

LEFT: Êdouard Chimot, *Pussy-Cats,* 1932

BELOW: Anonymous, *The Memories of a Prostitute* (Paris: Privately Printed, 1926)

If we accept the mock-serious commentary, sexist caricatures, and snarky photomontages in Paris' men's magazines, the once lofty expanse between ladies of unblemished morality — the weddable sorts — and their trampy cousins had receded in the postwar years and virtually collapsed. All women in the City of Love were perceived as head-turning vipers. At least, the sex-for-pay escorts offered a straightforward exchange of goods. And they were, in the end, far less demanding or costly.

PROSTITUTES AND STREETWALKERS

Basil Woon estimated that there were over 70,000 prostitutes working the streets, first-floor studios, and apartment houses of Paris in 1925. His account of this rollicking scene (*The Paris That's Not in the Guide Books* (New York: Robert M. McBride & Co., 1926) did not include the employees of the more formal and licensed venues — the 220 brothels. Those institutions increased the aggregate of female sex-workers by approximately 10%. (The official assessment by the city's Vice Commissioner was between 25,000 and 30,000 women. But few journalists accepted his lowball figure.)

The more brazen independents advertised their services in entertainment journals and cheap risqué weeklies. The back pages of these throwaway broadsheets were principally devoted to this explicit pleasure-market. Overall, some 350 prostitutes announced their availability in these listings, complete with telephone numbers and directions from the closest Métro station. Sometimes they disguised their clandestine intentions with promises of "worldly unions," "Greek bathing,"

PARISIAN PROSTITUTE TYPES

AMAZONES: Hefty sirens. Frequently serviced clients in the back of automobiles.

BELLES DE JOUR ("Beauties of the Day"): Discreet, part-time call girls from good backgrounds. Often housewives working in secret. [Variant name: *Demi-castors*.]

BERGERONETTES ("Wagtails"): One-legged whores.

BUCOLIQUES: Freelancers who stationed themselves in parks.

CANAILLE ("Trash"): Lowest order of streetwalkers.

CASSE-NOISETTES ("Nut-crackers"): Prostitutes whose vaginas had the contractile strength of a hand.

CHANDELLES ("Candles"): Itinerant bombshells who appeared at set times in front of bars or tourist hotels.

CHOUETTES ("Little Cabbages"): Number One Girls of the mecs. [Variant names: *Marmites* ("Stewing Pots") or *Girondes* ("Tender Ones").]

CLANDESTINES: Unlicensed hookers. [Variant name: *Insoumises*.]

COURTISANES: Exclusive kept ladies. High-end and glamorous. [Variant names: *Caravelles* or *Demimondaines*.]

ECHASSIÈRES ("Long-legged Birds" or "Stilt Walkers"): Indoor prostitutes who sat on elevated barstools in order to show off their silk-stockinged legs.

ENTÔLEUSES: Bottom-of-the-rung whores who picked the pockets of the *michés*. Usually worked in pairs. While one serviced the customer, the other emptied his wallet.

ÉTOILES FILANTES ("Shooting Stars"): Young, enticing maidens on the make.

FEMMES DE RESTAURANT: Prostitute-waitresses.

FILLES À NUMÉRO: Licensed streetwalkers. [Variant name: *Filles en carte*.]

FILLES DE CHAMBRE: Hotel prostitutes.

FILLES DE JOIE ("Daughters of Joy"): Generic term for all manner of prostitutes.

FILLES DE MAISON: Brothel girls.

FLEURS ("Flowers"): Les Halles floozies who awoke at dawn in order to solicit off-duty forts (porters).

FOURNISSEURS ("Suppliers"): Retinue of pensionnaires in a brothel.

GOUGNETTES: Lesbian prostitutes.

GRISETTES: Teenage vixens, generally found in the Latin Quarter. [Prewar term.]

HIRONDELLES ("Swallows"): Independents who lured men by sitting in front of the windows of their apartments.

HORIZONTALES: Indiscriminate whores. [Pejorative slang.]

HÔTEL LIMPETS ("Hotel Mollusks"): Unscrupulous harpies who plied their trade on foreign tourists.

IRRÉGULIÈRES: Manicurists, masseuses, and amateurs who engaged in paid sex. [Variant name: *Occasionalles*.]

LOLLIPOPS: Underage prostitutes. [From the English.]

MARCHEUSES: Streetwalkers. [Variant name: *Radeuses de nuit*.]

MIDINETTES: Hard-partying, working-class tarts.

MONTMARTROISES: Late-night predators from Pigalle.

NON-SÉRIEUSES: Pavement-pounders, usually addicts, controlled by small-time *souteneurs*.

PETITES FEMMES: Pretty, dolled-up women who sat patiently in café corners or bars for gentlemen on the lowdown.

PETITES GRUES ("Little Cranes"): Timid or naïve prostitutes. [Variant name: *Petites poules* ("Chicks").]

PIERREUSES ("Stones"): Old or diseased whores who masturbated their clients on the curbsides of Les Halles.

POULES ("Chickens"): Fresh-faced prostitutes.

POULES DE LUXE ("Sumptuous Chickens"): Expensive ladies from the Champs-Élysées.

SÉRIEUSES: Mature damsels who enacted sadist scenes in brothels.

SPÉCIALISTES: Professional dominatrices.

TROTTOIRS ("Sidewalks"): Over-the-hill or hideous-looking hustlers. [Pejorative slang.]

TAXI-GIRLS: Attractive mannequins who were selected by gentlemen at fancy nightclubs and paid in coupons for each dance. Generally considered to be late-night pickups.

VIOQUES: Old harlots.

VISITEUSES: Polite term for *Rendez-vous* ladies.

ABOVE: Brassaï, *Prostitute Playing Billiards at a Boîte on Boulevard Rochechouart*, 1932

OPPOSITE: *Le Sourire* (October 17, 1929)

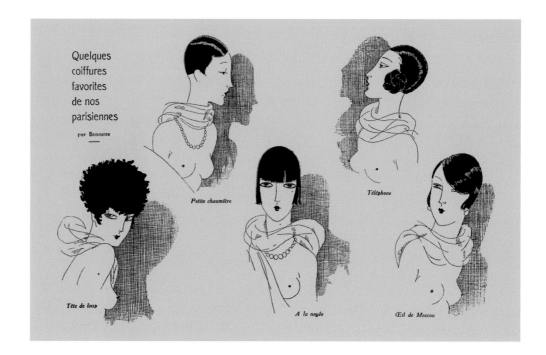

ABOVE: *A* Marcheuse *Near the Place de la République*, 1925

RIGHT: Léon Bonnotte, *Some of the Favorite Hairstyles of Our Parisiennes*, 1925

BELOW: Marco Laboccetta, *School for Gigolos*, 1924

OPPOSITE: Léon Fontan, *The Echassière Dangles Her Bait*, 1928

"society marriage," "sensational curiosities," "transformations," "intimate fortune-telling," "full-body massages," or, bizarrely, "midwifery."

The vast majority of prostitutes and streetwalkers eschewed the printed word. They dressed in full whorish display and positioned themselves in obvious locales where the traffic in single males or tourists was brisk and unimpeded. Most *filles de joie* arranged permanent ports of call in seedy cafés or lampposted corners. They were barely visible to the shopkeepers, neighborhood residents, and foot police.

Any taxonomical depiction of the typical Parisian hooker proved to be a stupefying challenge for the interwar abolitionists and social engineers. First, there were tens of thousands of wayward women active at any one time and they came from jarringly divergent backgrounds. Many were born into the unvirtuous trade; some girls abandoned their bourgeois households for underworld adventure; still others, already damaged goods, fled from peasant or working-class communities far from Paris or France. (For instance, after the Falangist victory in 1939, multihued throngs of Spanish brothel-workers suddenly materialized on the streets of Pigalle.)

Nearly every nocturnal *fille* — for reasons of age, upbringing, physical appearance, training, ethnicity, and professional association — evolved into a distinctive type. Many were known for their specific erotic skills or inviting domiciles. Certain habituées attired themselves as fantasy playmates: there were pretend adolescent bad girls, smutty sisters, frustrated Catholic-school teachers, mistresses, two-timing wives, and wizened stepmothers and grandmothers.

A FRIEND: "Careful, Suzy, your legs will ignite your next client!"

SUZY: "That's my intention! Let him explode in his pants. It saves me from standing up."

de la
courtisane

de la midinette

For the stables of *montmartroises* controlled by the *souteneurs* (or pimps), however, roleplay was an impediment to speedy transactions, if altogether superfluous. The unadulterated lure was bargain-basement BJs and feral coupling. Neither the streetwalkers nor their besotted prey had the means or time for imaginative foreplay. Mute porcine rutting was the draw.

CRITICAL RESPONSE AND ABOLITION

The obvious effects of prostitution on family life and Parisian women were difficult to assess. Few wives or mistresses publicly complained. If the cavorting was executed in a prudent manner, the results appeared pretty much inconsequential. It certainly provided sybaritic innovations in middle-class boudoirs and enhanced ladies' daring sense of fashion. (Brassaï later maintained that the mini-skirts and thigh-high boots of the 1960s were merely *jeunes* retreads of thirties *Fleur* wardrobe.)

The movement to outlaw commercialized sex had its vociferous advocates within French feminist organizations, the parties of the religious right, and among the leaders of rival reactionary and Communist circles. Yet, the political crusade to end legal prostitution did not pick up steam until after Allied armies liberated Paris in August 1944. ⚜

OPPOSITE, CLOCKWISE FROM TOP LEFT: Jack Abeille, *The Mirror of the Courtisane*, 1932; Lindel, *The Non-Sérieuse Gets Her Reward* (a packet of cocaine), 1927; Jack Abeille, *The Mirror of the Midinette*, 1932; Jihet, *A Chandelle on Rue Blondel*, 1946; Jeanne Mammen, *Dogdays* (Two *Petites Femmes*), 1925

ABOVE: *The* Bergeronette *Limps into View*, 1928

LEFT: Léon Fontan, Fournisseurs *at Chez Christiane*, 1933

CLOCKWISE FROM TOP LEFT: Zellé, *The Sérieuse Breaks Her Steed*, 1930; *Fleurs* on a Les Halles Thoroughfare, 1946; Taxi-Girls at Le Coliséum, 1933; A Bevy of *Clandestines* Off the Rue Saint-Denis, 1945

OPPOSITE: Two *Radeuses de Nuit* on Pont Alexandre by the Seine, 1939

THE FLESHPOTS OF MONTMARTRE AND LES HALLES

> *In Montmartre, the most serious people occasionally behave in an unexpected way, while no one seems to pay any attention to what anyone else may do.*
>
> — Ralph Neville, *Days and Nights in Montmartre and the Latin Quarter*, 1927 —
>
> *Montmartre, the summit of naughtiness. Babylon with the lid off.*
>
> — James Graham, *Montmartre — Playground of the World*, 1927 —

DAYTIME: IN THE SHADOW OF THE SACRÉ-CŒUR

OPPOSITE: Brodsky, *Chez Florence, Where the Dance Never Ends*, 1935

I N 1860, THE WALL SEPARATING *la Butte Montmartre* from Paris proper was unceremoniously torn down and removed. As a security precaution, the city council had voted to extend its northernmost boundary and annex the picturesque hillside village. The densely populated capital now had acquired enough land to create two new *arrondissements*.

Montmartre's premodern history was largely tethered to religious and military conflict. Its summit once buttressed a temple of Mars. The Pope's emissary, Saint Denis, erected a chapel over its ruins. The beheading of him and two of his assistants at the hands of the pagan Decians in 250 A.D. later gave rise to its current name — the Mount of Martyrs. (The hardy bishop was said to have picked up his severed head and ambled six miles northward, preaching and making converts on the way.)

Monasteries and a sacred cemetery were built on Montmartre's knolls and plains. Clay quarries provided ample material for the restoration of its churches that were repeatedly laid waste during the Dark Ages. French and Norman armies fought intermittent battles to secure its strategic heights. Over the centuries, fires, sectarian skirmishes, and workers' revolts devastated the communal institutions of Montmartre but the land was fertile and its citizens resolute.

With the end of the Napoleonic epoch, however, the place had received a doubtful reputation. Its quaint taverns and public houses were known for their local brews and accessible servant girls. And after the German High Command entered Paris at the conclusion of the Franco-Prussian War in 1871, Montmartre's plateau became the staging ground for the last nineteenth-century revolution, the Paris Commune. The Anarchist-Socialist insurrection lasted exactly two months. National troops from Versailles overwhelmed the Communards in a series of massacres that cost over 30,000 lives.

ABOVE: Bouxin, *A Montmartre Repast*, 1934

Partly to compensate for the unprecedented citizen slaughter and mass executions, construction of a monumental national shrine, the Basilica of the Sacré-Cœur, commenced four years later. By the time the neo-Byzantine complex was completed in 1914, Montmartre had incongruously established itself as the city's Bohemian playland, attracting flocks of avant-garde painters, loose women, balladeers, poets, and fun-seekers. Devout Catholic pilgrims from the hinterlands brushed shoulders with whoremongers who positioned themselves in the winding pathways of consecrated Pigalle.

EVENING TO 2 A.M.:
THE KINGDOM OF CHAMPAGNE

DANCINGS

Three dance halls in Montmartre predated the Great War. Two of them catered exclusively to locals but the third, the *Bal Tarabin*, grew exponentially in importance and was the harbinger of the brash tourist industry that cropped up after the Armistice. It provided several different kinds of erotic diversions in one luxurious

three-storied palace. In the basement was a strip joint known as the *Paradise*. In the main and top floors, diners could wiggle their way from nightclub stalls to the spacious dance arena, to a crowded American bar counter, or to the intimate seclusion of one of two balconies.

The central mahogany platform was designated for ballroom dance in the early evening and, after midnight, for eight leggy revue sketches, including girl-on-girl wrestling matches. When the mood dropped between cabaret *attractions*, young women in the balcony would routinely unbutton their blouses to reveal their exposed upper torsos. The appreciative spectators invariably greeted this with approving hoots and applause.

On Saturdays, the notorious *Triomphe de Vénus* was slated as the bacchanalian endpiece. English-language tourist guides never failed to marvel at the weekend free-for-all. (*Très jolie*.) Garlanded satyr-boys carried wooden platforms, decorated with artificial roses, to the center showground. Standing or sitting on each of the

ABOVE: Jean Dulac, *Le Triomphe de Vénus at the Bal Tarabin*, 1927

LEFT: Teddy Piaz, *The New Season at the* Bal Tarabin, 1934

RIGHT: Brücken, *Cancan Dancers at the* Bal Tarabin, 1936

six floats was a bare-breasted maiden in pseudo-Greek attire. As soon as the orchestra sounded a dissonant chord, Vénus and her entourage broke from their bas-relief poses and flung colored streamers and cloth-balls at the audience. These missiles were normally tossed back at the girls or at other celebrants.

Billed as the "Cosmopolitan Temple of Fantastic Dance," the Tarabin revived and updated the *cancan*, that signature girly salute from the *Belle Époque*. Although created down the street at the Moulin Rouge in 1889, the cancan was already a hackneyed representation of the Lautrec era. (Originally it was a vibrant and lewd takeoff of an eighteenth-century court box-dance, the *quadrille*.) The Tarabin choreographers modernized its appeal with sleeker performers, more revealing costumes, glossier hosiery, and Charleston-like orchestrations. Now the cancan leg-thrusts, pigeon wings, high-kicks, and 180-degree splits exposed a magnanimous sampling of female flesh in a decidedly mock nostalgic mode.

And like the old Moulin, the Bal Tarabin propelled the downtown socialite world into the whorish dregs of Pigalle. Its modest five-franc admission and informal dress code also drew French working-class couples, typists, bowler-hatted *roués*, clerks, and shopgirls as well as foreign tourists on holiday. And, of course, the *marcheuses* were plentiful. A *public mélangé*.

Exactly at three in the morning when the orchestra was packing up, both the streetwalkers and chorus girls pursued any unattached males. The harried clash over who would escort which clueless *miché* to her apartment was widely considered the most climactic moment in the toes-to-the-stars evening.

The Russian Revolution and World War radically altered the composition of immigrant Paris. The number of Russian speakers swelled from a statistically negligible community of 4,000 in 1914 to ten times that amount seven years later. The newest expats were mostly former aristocrats, mercantile families, and ex-officers from the battered White armies. Many fled their homeland with little more than suitcases, military regalia, sable coats, and jewels hidden in their undergarments.

Stateless and unaccustomed to the vicissitudes of exile, the Russian émigrés established neighborhoods in the suburbs and outlying districts. The most enterprising among them created Russian-themed restaurants, cabarets, and nightclubs. By 1925, a dozen such endeavors surfaced in Montmartre. One in particular, the *Château et Caveau Caucasiens*, proved to be a Parisian smash. It was an exotic and swanky imitation of the Bal Tarabin.

Founded by a Greek-American, the Caucasien mined the fascination for regal (class-conscious but not in the Bolshevik sense) entertainment, patrician elegance, and novel Russian cuisine. Like the Tarabin, each of its three floors conjured up an

ABOVE: Jean Dulac, *Château et Caveau Caucasiens*, 1927

independent fantasy environment: a downstairs Gypsy tavern, a Czarist-styled ballroom-dining hall, and upstairs cabaret. The Caucasien also cast a feudal wet dreamscape over its high-stepping clientele.

Besides the available *filles de joie* waiting at the in-house bars, doe-eyed Slavic beauties in peasant outfits seated themselves at the sightseers' tables. There, like implacable and parched-mad orphans, they pleaded for Champagne accompaniments. At 250 *francs* per bottle, it was the most profitable scam in Pigalle.

Popular Argentine culture slipped into Montmartre before the Great War. South American playboys, flush with wads of inflated *pesos* and *reals*, introduced the tango and its milonga instruments to the city's dance halls in the early 1900s. The first Latin tango dancers, however, had gained an unsavory status in their home country.

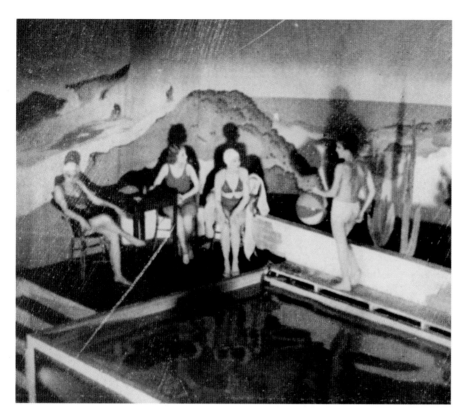

ABOVE: *The "Mermaids" of the Florida,* 1934

They were rumored to be lowlife denizens from the slaughterhouse district of Buenos Aires. In Argentina, the risqué — chest-to-chest and leg-wrapping — staccato-dances had been long associated with working-class taverns and brothels. By the time it arrived in Paris, the tango had shed its proletarian roots. It became the contemporary expression of chic-chic sophistication and graceful movement.

Several sumptuous *dancings* on Rue Blanche traded on the tango's enduring popularity. The ultra modern *Florida* claimed to be a replica of the Buenos Aires nightclub *Tabarys*. It had two orchestras, one for hot tangos and another for even faster-paced social dance. At the conclusion of the tangos, waiters handed out toy Indian dolls.

Where a cabaret podium normally would be mounted, the Florida installed a brightly illuminated fifty-foot tank of water for swimming and Deauville-like mayhem. There, six swim-suited "mermaids" lounged about, dove, and mimed water-polo matches. At the other end, a row of pomade-haired gigolos flashed knowing smiles at lonesome partners seeking a night of compassionate Spanish adulation. Exactly at midnight, the Argentine national anthem reverberated across the room; the crowd was expected to stand and sing along. Balloons were buffeted in the air and little orange cotton balls tossed at the mobile ceiling.

Nineteen twenty-one was the summer of jazz in Paris. Five American jazz bands — like Louis Mitchell's Jazz Kings, who were assembled from the remnants of Negro entertainment units in the American Expeditionary Force — set up camp in Montmartre's minuscule club spaces. Altogether, fifteen Harlem- or Plantation-motifed cabarets vied for top billing around Place Pigalle at the end of the decade.

Reoccurring images of African jungles, the antebellum South, and Manhattan skyscrapers floated before the adoring eyes of trendy French audiences. They were spellbound by the playful antics of the black musicians and conductor. While prewar ragtime and other American syncopated styles of "hot music" were rhythmic invitations to the floor dancers, with jazz, the orchestra itself created the kinesthetic spectacle; each performer manifested a spirited and boisterous personality with a distinct movement vocabulary of waves, flutters, nods, head shakes, bows, foot taps, winks, shoulder turns, and shuffles. The black musicians seemingly improvised gestures displayed something more than amusing physical banter; they would be the basis of a new art form, the Eccentric Dance.

To the cosmopolitan Frenchman, jazz not only invoked the timbre of a bewildering Americana but also gave a name to the era of social and sexual upheaval. Competing notions of the primitive and the modern, the drum and saxophone, the levee and the elevator strangely merged in the ubiquitous image of the dapper Negro jazzman. Jazz brought the aristocratic notion of fashion — monocles, tuxedoes, spats, jeweled tiaras and headbands, beaded slit dresses, silk stockings, and high-heeled pumps — into scandalous contact with the low culture of erotic black-American dance. For the deposed and the arriving European generations, jazz called out for an equality of pleasure, American optimism, surprise and mobility, the public display of forbidden desire, and an immediate international cult of youth.

Before the Wall Street Crash, French guidebooks claimed that *Chez Florence* was the "most sought-out cabaret" in Montmartre. Hotel brochures were even more animated: "The real, ripping hotsy-totsy place of Paris" and "an 18-karat diamond-studded sure thing."

No directions were needed to locate the tiny establishment on Rue Blanche; lines of limousines and hired cars packed the street directly in front of it and the attendant chauffeurs bounced to the pounding bass beat that trailed out of its doors. (In fact, the Chez Florence Jazz Band was so overpowering that inside the club, journalists enthused, "the joint shook like an explosion in the Métro.")

Dubbed *Chez Mitchell* after its owner, it was renamed in 1924 for the perky African-American personality Florence Embry Jones (1892–1932), who fancied snow-white evening gowns and demanded that all her tony patrons get up and wobble to the music. These included "all of Princeton, Yale, and Harvard," Rothschild-connected aristocrats, foreign royalty, American financiers, Arturo Toscanini, Argentinean bigwigs, and lots of black American expats. Chez Florence was also a good after-hours supper club that featured African-American treats,

like Chicken Maryland and poached eggs over corned beef hash, downed with compulsory Champagne or *très* expensive *vin*.

Her black MC, Frisco, a giant of a man, was an unequaled shouter, stepper, and vivacious showman. He pulled the dukes and duchesses out of their chairs and taught them how to roar into the Charleston, Black Bottom, and the latest tangos. Most showed their gratitude by plastering hundred-franc notes on his perspiring forehead.

Other African-American *dancings*, like *Bricktop's, the Big Apple, Plantation, La Jungle, Club Harlem, Dinah, Melody's Bar*, and the *Bal Nègre* featured authentic American jazz orchestras and interracial/transcontinental coupling. The Casino de Paris staged its elaborate idiosyncratic French version of the New World import in *Paris qui Jazz* and *Paris en l'Air*. Throughout the twenties and early thirties, porcelain figures of white Shimmy dancers and winking black musicians were much sought-after items in the galleries near the Odéon.

NIGHTCLUBS AND TOURIST TRAPS

ABOVE: Florence Jones behind the counter at *Chez Florence*, 1926

BELOW: Jean Dulac, *Le Canari*, 1927

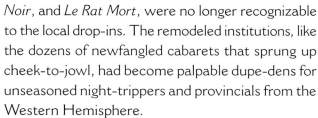

While foreign interlopers madly rummaged for inventive hooks that could ensnare Montmartre's free-spending tourist trade, over sixty nearby French cabarets and *dancings* stalked the very same Yankee dollar. The franc's worth had plummeted against most postwar currencies — and neophyte travelers liked what they heard about Paris. Revered bohemian haunts, such as *Le Lapin Agile, Le Chat Noir*, and *Le Rat Mort*, were no longer recognizable to the local drop-ins. The remodeled institutions, like the dozens of newfangled cabarets that sprung up cheek-to-jowl, had become palpable dupe-dens for unseasoned night-trippers and provincials from the Western Hemisphere.

In the heart of Montmartre, three peculiarly themed restaurant-cabarets opened for business in the 1890s and, over the decades, developed a startling cachet. The first, the *Cabaret du Néant*, was devoted to death and the disintegration of human cadavers — a bizarre topic for an eatery, to be sure, and a little downbeat for the comic proceedings. Yet the Néant's head-on gruesomeness proved to be its enduring attribute. Large, heavy wooden coffins, resting on biers, were set about the space as dining tables. The black drapery and grotesque positioning of real human skeletons on the walls suggested the aftermath of a frightful catastrophe or a dismembering station in a charnel-house. The guests even recalled a distinct graveyard odor that permeated its halls.

Cabaret du Néant

A black-caped *croquemort*, or hired pallbearer, ushers in the curious diners through a side door: "Welcome, O Weary Wanderer, to the Realm of Death! Enter! Choose your coffin, and be seated beside it!"

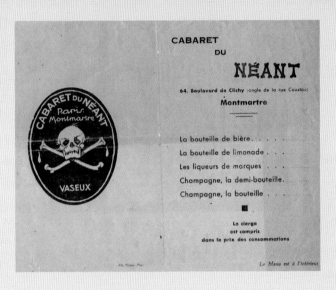

The gloomy "Room of Intoxication" is illuminated with a huge chandelier constructed with human bones and three skulls. The morbidly slow waiters are dressed as hearse drivers and describe each drink as a deadly contagion: cherry liquor as a glass of "malignant cancer," etc.

Then a black-frocked cleric, holding a thigh bone, reminds the patrons, whom he calls Coffin-Worms, of their impending doom and reels off the incredible varieties of dissolution that the Grim Reaper has planned for them. Their future is invariably Eternal Nothingness, the *raison d'être* of this macabre cabaret.

While he pontificates about their painful demises, glowing panels of frolicking men and music-hall dancers divulge their imminent fates as hideous cadavers. Other *objets d'art* include a bleeding neck from a guillotined victim and a laughing skull that flies through the air.

The monkish MC invites the revelers (for ten *francs*) into a dank passageway, "The Tomb of the Dead." As a harmonium wheezes off-key and funeral bells toll, three freshly deceased bodies pour out of an upright coffin.

One of them is a rosy-faced girl, who decomposes into a bald and fleshless corpse. A spectator is invited to stand in the coffin.

In a flash, his body transforms into skeletal remains. (All of these optical tricks are accomplished through mirrored projections, known as the "Pepper Effect.")

For another ten *francs*, the Coffin-Worms are brought into a third room, "The Gallery of Ghosts." There, an audience member is asked to sit on the stage. Unseen by him, a ghoulish spirit materializes. The mysterious phantom silently sets objects on an infant's coffin top. To the shill, they are totally invisible. (Again, the Pepper illusion.)

A female spectator is now cajoled to the backstage. Without any warning, her outer garments seem to vanish and she stands there in provocative underclothing. Of course, the female Worm is unaware of her immodest state and blankly stares back at the delighted audience.

As soon as the woman sits in the chair, her clothes instantly reappear. And the ghost returns to perform more tricks, like pulling a petrified rabbit from the empty coffin. This part of the show continues for ten more minutes.

When the crowd files out of the cabaret, they are encouraged to drop coins or bills into an inverted skull, which will insure them of a longer life on this earth.

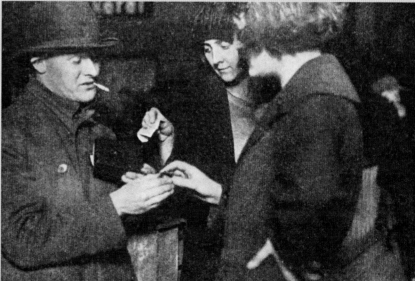

Across the street were the *Cabarets du Ciel et de L'Enfer*. These adjoining establishments relegated the vague afterworlds of Heaven and Hell into cartoonish fairylands.

In the Ciel, decrepit old waiters, *"garçons* of heaven," were costumed as white-robed angels with wire halos affixed to their blonde wigs. They responded to drink orders with mad benedictions, "Thy will be done!" Actors costumed as St. Peter (holding a four-foot Key to the Pearly Gates), Dante, and Father Time played their roles as *conférenciers* and guides.

Downstairs in the "Inner Sanctum," female angels in various states of undress seemingly flew across the room. This preceded other visions of "Mahometan Paradise and Oriental ecstasy." One gyrating female angel spun about attached to a cord and rested her hand on the most timid of the male spectators. Afterwards he was invited to a table on the rostrum and served a drink. What he could not see was the naked hostess who brought him the glass and then expressed her indignation at his lack of tactile interest.

The Cabaret de L'Enfer was a flipped vision of the Ciel with a bubbling caldron of musicians and hellish figures in the dining hall. After thirty minutes of demonic repartee, the Mephisto character led the diners into an upstairs auditorium. There, the spectators were greeted by his diabolic consort, Titania, and subjected to witnessing hysterical scenes of "eternal damnation" and the deadly sins that cast the reprobates into Hell.

ABOVE LEFT: Façades of the Cabarets *Le Ciel* and *L'Enfer* (Heaven and Hell), 1931

ABOVE RIGHT: Images of the *Cabaret du Ciel*, 1917

ABOVE: Images from the *Cabaret de L'Enfer*, 1917

BELOW LEFT: Henri Mahé, *From a Mural at the Bal Balajo*, 1936

BELOW RIGHT: Jeanne Mammen, *She and Her Friends*, 1914

The trio of cabarets equally mocked clerical notions of upright behavior and the prospects of otherworldly salvation. Additionally, they utilized similar comic tricks and received nearly identical responses to their comic homilies: the happily spooked patrons stamped their feet in approval while many French families departed in a huff midway through the sacrilegious burlesques.

BETWEEM 2 A.M. AND DAWN: THE CITADEL OF APACHEDOM

During the 1880s, the number of criminal gangs in Paris, always a visible street presence, appeared to grow precipitously — at least, in the eyes of the *Sûreté*, the police department's fabled detective division, and their reporter friends who

pumped out stories in the yellow press. By the turn of the century, the loose bands of thugs, burglars, pimps, and pickpockets in Montmartre and Les Halles had developed a common look and definable subculture. They were designated *apaches*. French journalists labeled them in order to distinguish the Parisian street hooligans from similar delinquent mobs in Marseille and Lyons, known as *nervis* ("edgy ones") or *kangourous* ("kangaroos").

The "apache" tag, which was happily received, marked the louts and their accomplices as a fierce variety of noble savage, like their Wild West namesake. Despite their antisocial and independent outlooks, the apaches shared a code of honor, recognizable dress, glossary of complex folkways, and enigmatic slang. For instance, in their parallel universe, fellow thieves never stole from one another and knife fights could only be conducted directly between the wronged parties, *mano a mano*. Typically, apaches donned workers' caps; they and their girlfriends (*blanchisseuses*) fancied red neckerchiefs — these hid the males' meticulously shaved necks. For the most part, apaches were known for their brutal treatment of their female partners and no *blanchisseuse* in good standing would ever allow her man to engage in lawful employment.

Verlan, the apache jargon, normally replaced the first letter of a word with an "l," moved the initial letter to the end; this was followed with a suffix. (The name "verlan" itself was a backwards term for "reverse.") More intriguing for outsiders, the apache *lingua franca* contained hundreds of invented expressions.

ABOVE: Fabius Lorenzi, *A Visit to the Bal-Musette*, 1925

BELOW: Henry Fournier, *Apache Beating for Spectators*, 1927

PARISIAN CRIMINAL ARGOT

ALPHONSES: Pimps. [Variant name: Louises. [*Fin-de-siècle* terms.]

APACHES: Street thugs and delinquents from Montmartre and Les Halles. [Variant name: Flies.]

BAG: One thousand *francs*. [From the English.]

BALS-MUSETTES: Cheapest dance halls with accordion bands; Apache hangouts.

BARBEAUX ("A Fresh-Water Fish With Barbs"): Pimps. [Variant names: *Barbillons* ("Fish-hooks"), *Harengs* ("Herrings"), *Poissons* ("Fish") and *Saurs* ("Kippers").]

LA BASTOCHE: Area around the Bastille, where the bals-musettes proliferated.

BISNESSE: Place of prostitution. [Corruption of the English word "Business."]

COCO: Cocaine.

CONFITURE ("Jam"): Narcotics.

DEMI-SELS ("Salted cheeses"): Small-time pimps.

ENTREMETTEURS ("Matchmakers"): Advancemen for streetwalkers. Mostly old Polish Jews in bowler hats.

FLICS: Policemen. [Ungrammatically used for a single patrolman.] [Variant names: *Argousins*, *Poulets* ("Chickens"), *La Rousse*, and *Vaches* ("Cattle").]

GANGSTERS: Organized criminals. [From the English.]

HÔTELS: Prisons. [Variant name: *Poplavilles* ("Henhouses").]

MACQUEREAUX ("Mackerels"): Generic term for pimps. [Abbreviated usage: "Macs" or "Mecs."]

MARLEUS: Gangsters from Les Halles.

MICHÉ: Purchased information.

MOUTONS ("Sheep"): Agent provocateurs planted by the police.

MRECS: Lesbian pimps.

NAZES: Syphilitics. [Variant name: Nazis.]

NUMÉROS: Scoundrels who initiated young girls into the trade.

PÈGRE: The underworld.

PISTEUR: Nagging information that prostitutes try to ignore.

PLACEURS ("Agents"): Procurers. Often enticed provincial women into leaving their families for a life in Parisian brothels. [Variant name: *Proxénètes*.]

SOUTENEURS: Violent pimps who maintained a stable of prostitutes.

TAULIERS ("Bosses"): Proprietors of unregistered brothels. [Variant name: *Tôliers*.]

TRIPOTS: Gambling dens.

TRUANDS: Roughnecks.

LA VEUVE ("The Widow"): The guillotine.

VOYOUS: Common thugs.

ZINCS: Saloons.

The ornate mores and expressive culture of the apaches increasingly captivated the attentions of well-born Parisians and intrepid tourists. They frequented the downtrodden dance halls, known as *bals-musettes*, in *la Bastoche* and even paid dearly to watch them "perform" in phony, if safer, venues. The anthropological thrill of witnessing violent underworld and lowlife sexuality did not disappoint. Montmartre and Les Halles had created another novel choreographic attraction. Besides street prostitution and *dancings*, there were now intimate displays of erotic primitivism.

APACHE SEX

The sexual lifestyle of the apaches appeared to resemble that of outlaw societies in other European cities: despite an immense public and artistic interest, it was veiled and, for the most part, even more unglamorous than the ugly exposés of it that were splashed across the pages of the crime weeklies and pulp press.

According to investigations by the Parisian *Service des Mœurs* (Bureau of Vice), few marcheuses

experienced any orgasmic pleasure from the dalliances with their *michés* or apache handlers. Most streetwalkers came from families where sexual gratification had been maniacally fused with nighttime molestation, abject cruelty, dominance, mother-daughter rivalry, and the childhood pairing of psychological humiliation and revenge. The *blanchisseuses* were eminently skilled in re-enacting the shifting roles of victim or abuser.

In their private lives, many — possibly most — apaches enjoyed the erotic companionship with individuals of their own sex. At least 40% of the incarcerated females acknowledged to the *agents des mœurs* that their primary affairs were with lesbian acquaintances. At certain *bals-musettes*, male apaches publicly danced groin-to-groin with their favorite comrades-in-arms. These same-sex attachments were rarely secretive or thought to be on the down-low because neither partner considered himself to be a "queen" or effeminate. (And since each party behaved as an active seducer, both were accorded the status of manly heterosexuals.)

ABOVE: Henry Fournier, *Apache Beating for Spectators*, 1927

BELOW: Carlos d'Eschevannes, *A Pimp from the Milieu* (Paris: Privately Printed, 1930)

Drugs also fueled the economy of desire in the apache constellation. Anxious *trottoirs* lingered in the backrooms of hawk-faced dealers for their early-morning fixes. Cocaine, morphine, heroin, and hashish were commonly exchanged for sex, no questions asked. Discarded square glassine envelopes and broken glass vials littered the alleys and curbsides of Montmartre and Les Halles.

RUE LAPPE AND ITS *BALS-MUSETTES*

The *bals-musettes* around the Place de la Bastille became the heart and life-blood of Apachedom. Not only were they the punks' hub of amusement, the *bals* functioned as neutral assembly zones. "Civilians" wandered the front dance areas; *bisnesse* was conducted at the bar counters or under the elevated orchestra balconies; and *le Milieu*, the fraternity of white-slave traffickers, maintained padlocked quarters in back-of-the-store dwellings. Human barter, gang discipline, undercover commerce, trial and punishments, as well as evocative dance, all took place under one roof.

LEFT AND BELOW: Germaine Krull, *The Vrais de Vrais*, 1933

The *bals* themselves began innocently. At the tail end of Napoleon's reign, country immigrants from the South-Central region of Auvergne recreated their hard-drinking folk celebrations in the *Bastoche's* antiquated bistros. The merry-making Auvergners added Italian accordion players to their bands of picturesque bagpipers, violinists, and guitar players. This feral new music suited the apaches and was perfect for squashed and sexy versions of the polka and waltz. (Men often guided their partners by placing both hands on their buttocks.) Ultimately, it produced the apaches' own fast-paced dance, the *java*, a rumba-like anything-goes tango-ette.

By 1928, the *Service des Mœurs* listed over 165 late-night *bals-musettes*. On the cobblestoned Rue Lappe alone, there were seventeen such establishments. And celebrated French recording artists churned out hundreds of java hits. Pop Gallic culture had finally locked arms with apache criminality. The heady concoction lasted until German censors put an end to them in 1940. ✤

MAISONS CLOSES

See all, hear all, but say nothing.
— Motto of the Sphinx Brothel, 1930 —

The steady clientele of a closed house was very loyal to it, and you didn't even have to open your fly. You'd drink a brandy or cosy around a table, smoking and making small Frenchy jokes, mostly about priests and water closets, or General Joffre's cock. What gave it away as a snatch shop was the girls were mostly naked, or just wearing stockings and high-heeled slippers, a bit of lace, and they were singing "J'aime à jamais."
— W.W. Windstaff, *Lower Than Angels*, 1931 —

CHAPTER

4

THE SEEMINGLY NEVER-ENDING STREAM of migrants from the countryside into European and American cities during the nineteenth century utterly transformed the trade in commercial sex. The colossal surge in prostitution and white slavery potentially threatened the health, public safety, deference to civic authority, and social climate of urban life. Most industrialized nations and municipalities had to implement draconian laws and shore up regulatory agencies to control, delimit, and police it. But vast cultural, religious, and regional differences ensured that no single edict or decree could be effectively applied.

OPPOSITE: A *Scène Lubrique* in *L'Acropole*, 1930

Even neighboring ports had divergent and contentious traditions. Some cities and towns restricted otherwise illicit activities to "red zones," outlawed them entirely, curbed them only among targeted groups, or paid no particular heed to their unruly existence.

Paris, of course, devised a unique solution. In the late 1820s, the 180 independent brothels, scattered across its *arrondissements*, were licensed and "legalized." Over the next 120 years, various pieces of legislation mandated the hygienic conditions, appearance, placement, and ownership requirements. Sex-workers had to be inspected for venereal disease at least twice each month. The city-approved bordellos could not advertise their presence with indiscreet signage or garish symbols. They had to be located on a side street, away from any central boulevard and more than one hundred meters from any recognized school or church. Curiously, only women could officially run or own the brothels. And not just any females: the title-holders of the "shuttered houses" had to be former prostitutes who were currently married.

The *maisons closes* proved to be immensely profitable, directly employing over seven thousand Parisiennes, with thousands more working in allied services, like interior design, accounting, food preparation, bartending, laundering, building maintenance, and publicity. Many wealthy, if anonymous, investors doubled and tripled their fortunes in this not quite laissez-faire industry. Unlike capital ventures in agriculture or mechanized industries, this had unlimited potential and government protection.

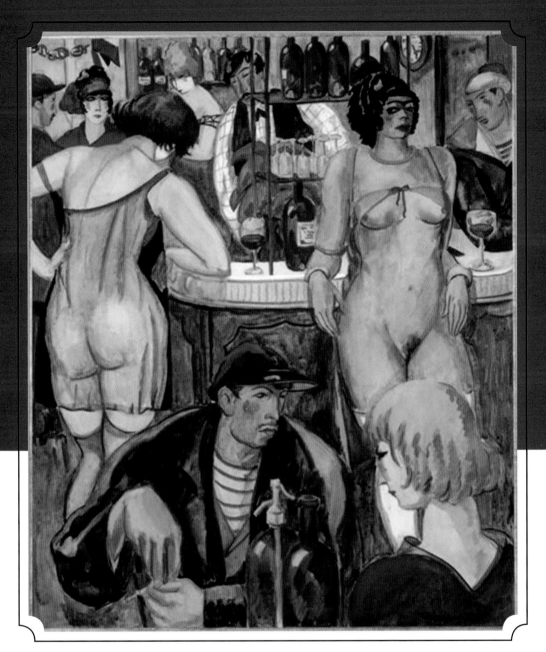

The classifications of the brothels in many ways resembled those of hotels or restaurants. In general, they were broken into three categories: mammoth luxury establishments, where customers might spend the better part of an evening (*maisons de tolérance*); intimate, more personal-sized dwellings (*maisons de rendez-vous*); and dirt-cheap lairs that mimicked the speed and efficiency of a factory assembly line (*maisons d'abattage*).

Annual directories and business cards advertised and updated the latest additions to the *maisons closes*. Smaller houses relocated with some regularity and, occasionally, the names of competing brothels — based on street addresses or landladies' nicknames — were confusingly duplicated. So there were multiple *Château d'Eau*s, *Chez Billy*s, Chez *Suzy*s, Le *Hanovre*s, *Le Panier Fleuri*s, and *Temples of Beauty*. Guidebooks, like the ubiquitous *Guide Rose* or *Guide-Indicateur des Maisons de Plaisirs et d'Art de Paris,* were essential aids.

TERMS FOR BROTHELS

BOÎTES DE NUIT ("Boxes of the Night"). Nocturnal establishments.

HÔTELS PARTICULIERS ("Special Hotels"). Dwellings that rented rooms for sexual contact.

MAISONS À GROS NUMÉRO: Brothels with a selection of many whores.

MAISONS DE CINQ HEURES ("5 O'Clock Houses"). *Maisons de rendez-vous*, usually with four to seven prostitutes. Sometimes advertised as Institutes of Beauty or Massage Salons.

MAISONS DISCRÈTES: Hidden brothels for clergy.

MAISONS OFFICIELLES: State-recognized brothels.

MAISONS DE PLAISIRS ("Houses of Pleasure"). Bordellos. [Variant names: *Bouges*, *Maisons à estaminet*, *Maisons publique*, and *Maisons de soulagement* ("Houses of Relief").]

MAISONS DE PASSE ("Houses of Call"). Whorehouses usually located, identified with a red lantern.

MAISONS DE SOCIÉTÉ: High-class brothels. [Variant names: *Cloaques* or *Maisons d'illusion*.]

MAISONS DES ILLUSIONS ("Houses of Illusion"). Brothels that specialized in roleplay. Frequently had peepholes and mirrored rooms.

PETITS SALONS: Prostitute apartments. [Variant name: *Résidences meublée* ("Furnished Rooms").]

SOINS ESTHÉTIQUES: Massage parlors that specialized in masturbation.

Maryse Choisy (1903–1979), arguably the most brazen and eccentric nonfiction author of the period, spent one month in 1927 professing to be a *fille de joie* in search of gainful employment. Her feigned undertaking allowed her to explore the inner workings of some fourteen Parisian brothels. During her four-week trek, the vixen-like Choisy (then a chiromanist, future Freudian psychotherapist, still later a newspaper-columnist philosopher with a Socratic bent, and finally a Christian mystic and yogi) interviewed dozens of madams and prostitutes with unflinching verve.

LEFT: Rudolf Matouschek, *The League of Nations in Paris*, 1927

Her book *A Month With the Girls* (Paris: Éditions Montaigne, 1928), a delirious anthropological saga, became an international best-seller. Several years later after the chastened occultist underwent a life-changing religious conversion, Choisy attempted to purchase and destroy all extant copies of her sociological masterwork.

MAISONS DE TOLÉRANCE

The term *maisons de tolérance* ("Houses of Tolerance") first appeared in print during the 1840s and referred to large-scale bordellos where the girls lived as full-time inhabitants. These massive cat-houses consisted of whole five-story buildings that included foyers, Selection Parlors, several floors of partitioned chamber-rooms, and secluded living quarters. With the founding of *Le Chabanais* in 1878, however, *maisons de tolérance* acquired an added meaning: plush, architecturally sumptuous venues that catered to an elite clientele.

BELOW: *Selection Salon,* 1900

Le CHABANAIS

LEFT: Roger, *The King and His Foreign Subjects*, 1903

Established by the "Irish-born Madame Kelly," *Le Chabanais* was the most opulent and politically savvy of the Parisian brothels. It was rumored to have cost the mind-boggling sum of 1.7 million *francs* when it opened. Naturally many of its high-ranking stakeholders cloaked their identities by registering as "George the Cavalry Officer" or "Pointy Nose."

From 1900 until the Colonial Exposition of 1937, French Interior Ministers commonly arranged sexual rendezvous at the Chab for official state guests under the guise of a "late-night visit with the President of the Senate." The Third Republic's onetime Foreign Minister, Louis Barthou, before his assassination in 1934, was a recurrent patron himself. A buxom *fille* led the conservative politician around the room like an obedient poodle and lashed his bare bottom when he dallied too long. His spiked collar and leash were accorded an honored position in the Chab's private trophy case.

The décor of Le Chabanais was astoundingly lavish and widely heralded in the press. Among its thirty private chambers and salons, there was a replica of a maharaja's palace suite; a Persian harem; a Moorish room (with a pool and tropical plants); a Czarist chamber (where clients could be disciplined with Russian knouts); a Spanish ward; a Japanese bedroom (with tatami matting, a bank of mirrors, and a woodblock panel of Mount Fuji); a Pompeii Room (filled with murals of Rome and Florence, with operatic arias piped in); American, Egyptian, and Venetian lounges;

ABOVE: Léo Fontan, *The Royal Bathtub*, 1932

BELOW: Edward VII's *Fauteuil d'Amour* or "love-throne."

as well as imitations of Louis XV and XVI's imperial salons. The Japanese room was so highly regarded that it received an award for Interior Design at the Universal Exhibition of 1900.

Madame Kelly pioneered the genteel selection process by arranging her assortment of *femmes galantes* in a darkened parlor setting. Each of the Chab's ladies was not only a familiar type (gracious music-hall *chanteuse*; demure provincial schoolgirl; sparkling conversant Jewess; sophisticated African princess; etc.) but groomed and coiffed to look like actual stars from the French stage and screen. Introductions in the parlor were socially circumspect and indirect. The secondary action upstairs, however, was less diplomatic and sometimes beyond the ken of ordinary nuptials.

During its first two decades, for example, the future King of England, Edward VII ("Bertie") frequented this tony establishment. The Hindu Chamber was redesigned as his private room, complete with a coat of arms hanging over the bejeweled Madras bed. Among the pieces of erotic furniture specially created for him was a copper bathtub in the shape of a giant swan-woman, which was filled with fine Champagne that he shared with several prostitutes. Throughout the thirties and forties this *objet d'art érotique* was prominently displayed in the foyer. In 1951, Salvador Dali purchased it for 112,000 *francs*.

Even more exotic was "Dirtie Bertie's" *fauteuil d'amour* or "love-throne." This curious upholstered and brass contraption was built in 1890 to make it possible for the obese Prince to mount his female companion without crushing her — granting him an unspoiled mechanical advantage. It also accommodated trios for simultaneous oral-anal encounters. The apparatus was, reportedly, utilized by the migratory heavyweights Fatty Arbuckle and Hermann Goering.

AUX BELLES POULES

Although utterly different in mood and appeal, the *Aux Belles Poules* was also listed as a *maison de tolérance*. Here the atmosphere radiated giddy laughter and smutty charades. The moment a customer entered the "Chicken Run," two or three playful *femmes* approached. On the ground floor, dozens of prostitutes in diaphanous slips or imitation leopard skins and high-heel pumps shared drinks with their potential clients. Many pranced about, naked from the waist down.

By the bar, girls competed in a game called the "Forty *Sous*." They picked up *jetons* or coins off the edge of coffee tables with their labia majora and deposited them into a moneybox. Others placed the tips of burning cigarettes or cigars in their vaginas and expelled smoke from them.

Looking for some outré erotic activity, Henry Miller brought Anaïs Nin here in February 1932 to witness a private lesbian performance. In the Red Chamber, a large Spanish prostitute strapped on a pink dildo and penetrated her tiny blonde female partner repeatedly. They shifted positions as soon as the dominant *gousse* shouted out an imaginary locale or situation: in the back of a taxicab; in the "Spanish manner" (between the breasts); against an outdoor wall, like desperate lovers who cannot afford a hotel room; and delicately from behind in order not to wake her sleepy bride.

Finally, the fat aggressive Spaniard orally stimulated her pliant partner until she achieved authentic orgasm.

ABOVE: Charles Laborde, *Aux Belles Poules*, 1926

BELOW: A *jeton* (or token) for sex, 1925

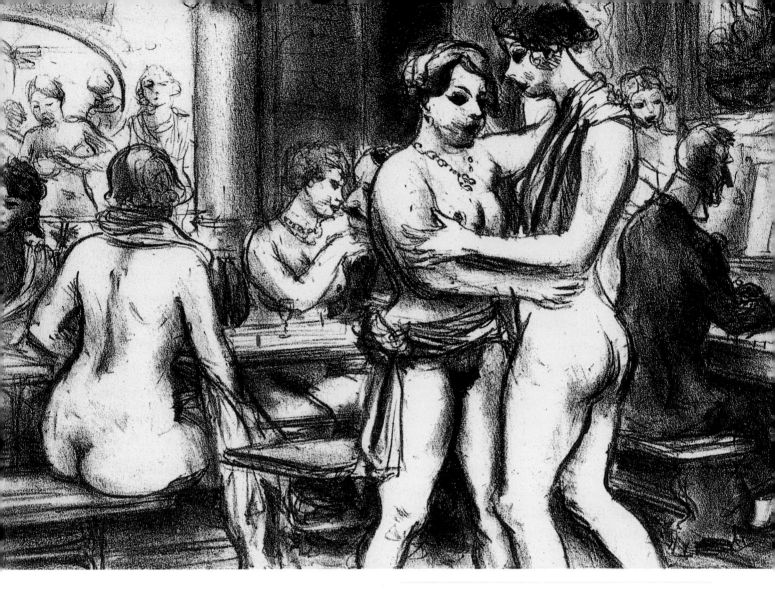

TOP: Reginald Marsh, *Aux Belles Poules*, 1928

BOTTOM: Fabienne and Marcel Jamet, 1935

ONE TWO TWO

Marcel and Fabienne Jamet opened the *One Two Two* in 1924. The Anglicized name not only related to its street address on Rue de Provence but was also a comic euphemism for visiting a brothel. When the dignitaries at the Jockey Club wanted to inform their peers, in front of their unsuspecting wives, that they intended to conclude the evening at a *maison de tolérance*, they merely announced in English, "Tonight, one ... and two ... and two."

The Jamets had a good business sense and were equally fun-loving. Fabienne's father was a retired *agent des mœurs* and helped her find fresh recruits for the sex work. Their brothel offered kitschy environments and fine dining. At the 122, one could really sexually transverse continents and eras — and then laugh about it over Champagne and tasty bistro fare.

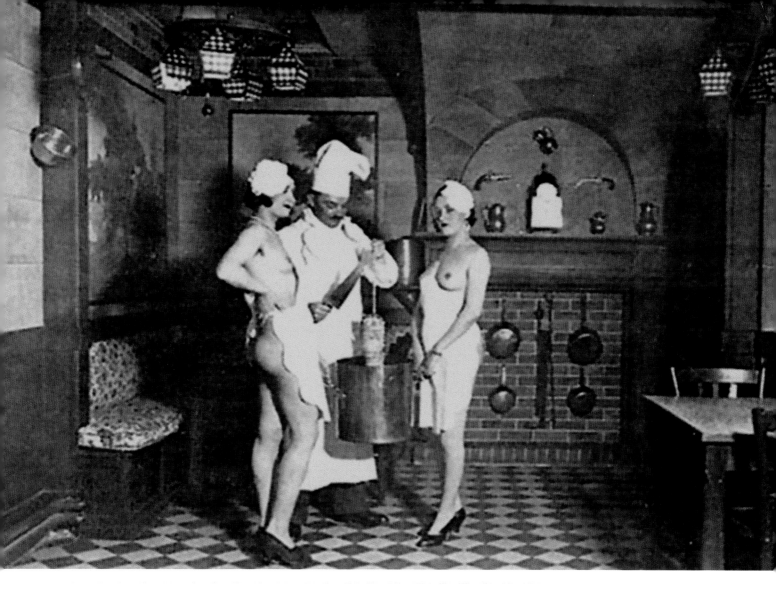

The Selection Parlor was a designed like an outdoor flower grotto with painted erotic scenes, marble columns, and a long, narrow Greek-like stage. Additionally, on its seven floors, there were over one dozen theme rooms. The imaginative chambers included a swaying Ocean Liner Compartment (a foghorn blew when the hour elapsed); an immaculate Torture Cell; a Provincial Rustic Lodge; a Chapel for Black Masses; an African Safari Hut; a Dining Hall (designed like an outdoor

ABOVE: The *122* underground kitchen

BELOW: Girls at dinner

ABOVE: The Miami Beach Dining Hall at One Two Two

BELOW: Brassaï, *Room of Mirrors*, 1932

Miami Beach lounge); a Pirate's Cabin; an Indian Room; a François I Boudoir; an igloo-like Arctic Salon, and two Rooms of Mirrors.

In the Orient-Express Couchette, which rocked, whistles were blown and moving pictures of landscapes unrolled outside an interior window-frame. Here the customer would find a saucy schoolgirl, engrossed in a book. During his faux seduction of the fascinating passenger, a second prostitute dressed as a ticket-taker slid open the door, catching them in *flagrante delicto* and completed their improvised *ménage-à-trois*!

A typical day at the 122 began at 2 p.m. and lasted until five in the morning. During that time, the fifty to sixty saucy girls normally serviced three hundred customers. The Jamets' motto was "Be punctual and remember the gentleman always comes first." Fabienne treated her employees well and trained them to be more like geishas than no-frills *fournisseurs*. Most were young and lighthearted to begin with.

Fabienne's clientele appreciated the homey atmosphere and, according to her postwar memoirs, included an array of prominent celebrities, notably members of the deposed Bourbon dynasty, Marlene Dietrich, Jack Warner, Mae West, Katharine Hepburn, Humphrey Bogart, Pierrot le Fou (France's Public Enemy #1), King Leopold of Belgium, Randolph Churchill (Winston's son), and the Archbishop of Paris. The latter reportedly frequented The One's Miami Beach restaurant for the savory stringed beef stew, the specialty of the house.

Sometimes whole families were greeted. Wives were placed in a special enclosed patio, where they were encouraged to read and gossip with the off-duty whores or among themselves.

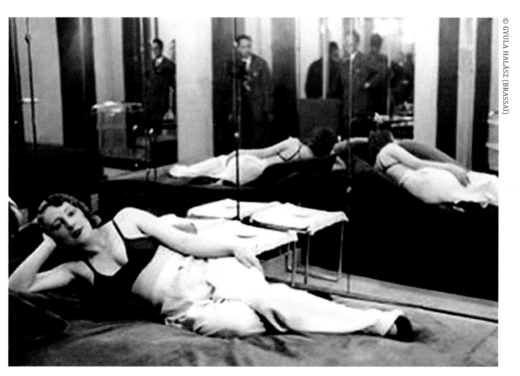

© GYULA HALÁSZ (BRASSAÏ)

✦ ONE TWO TWO Theme Rooms ✦

GREEK TEMPLE IN AN ENCLOSED GARDEN

INDIAN CHAMBER

TRANSATLANTIC OCEAN LINER

✦ ONE TWO TWO Theme Rooms ✦

BOUDOIR OF FRANÇOIS I

BLACK MASS CHAMBER

IGLOO

AFRICAN SAFARI HUT

Other *visiteurs*, however, proved more difficult. A maharajah from colonial India frequently corralled two or three *femmes* for the night but would get so wasted from the Champagne and frolicking that his glass eye would pop out. It later had to be returned to his suite at the Ritz. One high-profile prostitute, Blanche, still a virgin into her sixties, performed only for "princes or kings." Her expertise was flogging manacled royals in the Torture Chamber.

Lesser customers were also problematic. One regular hired a retinue of 122 *femmes de maison* to urinate on him. Fabienne had to install a room with water-proof carpeting. Another, known as the "wolf-man," took any available girl and, just before orgasm, jumped out of his room to howl in the corridors. A scandal sheet reported that almost one-third of the 122 customers were "Juicers," men who rushed into the prostitute's room after the last client exited and then sucked out the spent sperm from the girl's vagina or off her soiled lingerie.

Fabienne parsed the sexual vagaries of her international patrons. The British, naturally, demanded infantile punishments but delivered in a courteous manner. Americans were sexual ignoramuses; Germans, good-natured if inarticulate; Russians, wild-eyed brutes ("We don't pay capitalists; we hang them from lamp-posts!"); Italians, idiotic; Spaniards and South Americans, "libidinous quadrupeds." Worst of the all were the Japanese, who came to the 122 in packs of ten or twelve at a time and could never stop talking about the poor choices each made in the Selection Garden.

Frenchwomen were the most nonchalant. As long as their tumescent husbands left their secretaries alone, they didn't care how many 122ers they fornicated with. French mothers often initiated their teenage sons into manhood at The One. Some even sat in the chamber bedrooms, dispensing disapproving commentary as their boys prematurely climaxed.

LE SPHINX

Le Sphinx was probably the only *maison de tolérance* to have a public opening and proudly promoted itself as the most American in design and outlook. The Sphinx's primary inspiration was silent-movie Hollywood. Its founders, Georges Lemestre and his wife, Marthe (known as "Martoune"), had spent much of the twenties in

RIGHT: Sphinx Balcony,
undated;

OPPOSITE, LEFT TO RIGHT:
Sphinx *Pensionnaires*, 1935;
Sphinx Dining Hall, 1935;
Nielb, *Married Couples at
the Sphinx*, 1934

Prohibition America, befriending such cultural luminaries as Charlie Chaplin, Fatty
Arbuckle, Rudolph Valentino, and Al Capone. When they returned to Europe in
late 1929, it was still uncertain how much the Wall Street freefall would affect
the international markets and tourism.

Back in Paris, Martoune staked out the Left Bank for a classy and up-to-date
erotic citadel. Montparnasse's cache as an artistic destination had wilted over the
years and real estate was relatively cheap. The Lemestres with their suitcases of
dollars purchased a mason's loft next to a cemetery. Unlike most other *maisons de
tolérance,* the Sphinx was constructed in a unified and modernist style. Its five floors
alloyed toga-and-sword DeMille film set with functioning New York skyscraper.

After passing through a revolving door on Boulevard Edgar-Quinet, patrons
were exposed to a waterfall that flowed over a golden statue of the Egyptian
god Ptah. The dance floor and restaurant glistened. In fact, it was so bright and
waxy that journalists often compared the Sphinx to a late-night hospital dis-
pensary. Imported air-conditioning units, steel furniture, a high-fidelity speaker
system, and modern elevator lift completed the futuristic illusion.

Known as the "Queen of Nighttime Paris," Martoune hired *nues* and *figurantes*
from Pigalle revue houses and dressed them as *haute couture* hostesses. They were
reputed to be excellent conversationalists as well as amateur therapists. Politely,
a naked prostitute (with a purse covering her genitals) would sit at a family table
and address the wife or mistress if she could speak with the mister. If consent was
given, the new couple would exit to the elevator door and disappear. No brothel
allowed its *femmes* to present themselves in such a gracious or light-hearted style.

Customers queued up on the street. As many as 25% of the regulars came only for table service and playful *tête-à-têtes* with the prostitutes. Every Tuesday, badly wounded veterans of the Great War, the *grands blessés*, were given *carte blanche* treatment; Thursday was the day for graphic artists, who often traded drawings for free drinks and sexual engagements. To a large degree, the patrons created the entertainment, doing fast-draw sketches or devising amusing bar tricks. Souvenirs include erotic novelettes, ashtrays, *mosers* (the stirring rods for Champagne cocktails), and wine glasses all stamped with the Sphinx emblem. (A typical day realized 150,000 *francs* in profit.)

Children also encouraged their parents to take them to this New World establishment. A playroom filled with American toys and coloring books awaited the wide-eyed offspring. Innocent and corporal *plaisirs* beckoned the entire family. Astonishingly, some married couples rented empty bedrooms at the Sphinx and role-played an evening of limber prostitute and man-about-town *miché*.

With prosperity, political intrigue and petty corruption naturally followed. The *Sûreté* kept meticulous records about ministers and suspicious foreigners who frequented the place. It was rumored that undercover officials planned the mysterious and unsolved death of the con man Sacha Stavisky at the Sphinx. The Fascist *L'Action Française* attempted to disbar the brothel numerous times, claiming it was a hotbed of anti-French conspiracy. And Jean Cocteau maintained that Eva Braun visited Martoune's business premises in the mid-thirties and later convinced her Führer that *maisons* like this should be allowed to function in the New Europe.

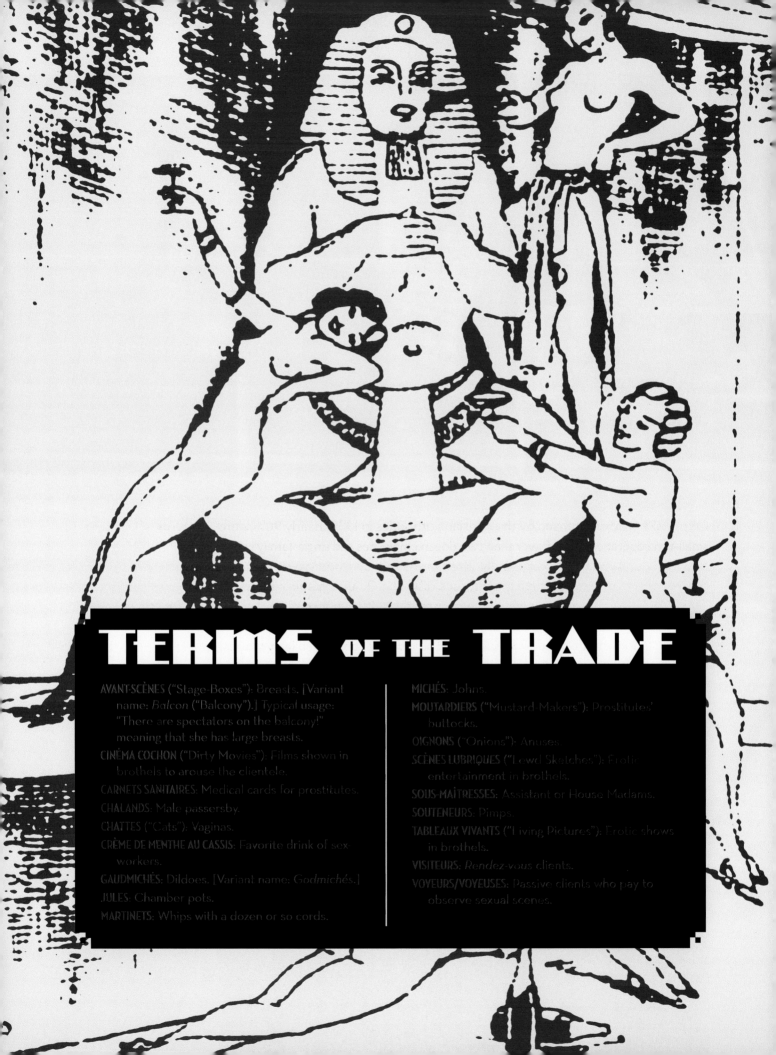

TERMS OF THE TRADE

AVANT-SCÈNES ("Stage-Boxes"): Breasts. [Variant name: *Balcon* ("Balcony").] Typical usage: "There are spectators on the balcony!" meaning that she has large breasts.

CINÉMA COCHON ("Dirty Movies"): Films shown in brothels to arouse the clientele.

CARNETS SANITAIRES: Medical cards for prostitutes.

CHALANDS: Male passersby.

CHATTES ("Cats"): Vaginas.

CRÈME DE MENTHE AU CASSIS: Favorite drink of sex-workers.

GAUDMICHÉS: Dildoes. [Variant name: *Godmichés.*]

JULES: Chamber pots.

MARTINETS: Whips with a dozen or so cords.

MICHÉS: Johns.

MOUTARDIERS ("Mustard-Makers"): Prostitutes' buttocks.

OIGNONS ("Onions"): Anuses.

SCÈNES LUBRIQUES ("Lewd Sketches"): Erotic entertainment in brothels.

SOUS-MAÎTRESSES: Assistant or House Madams.

SOUTENEURS: Pimps.

TABLEAUX VIVANTS ("Living Pictures"): Erotic shows in brothels.

VISITEURS: *Rendez-vous* clients.

VOYEURS/VOYEUSES: Passive clients who pay to observe sexual scenes.

MAISONS DE RENDEZ-VOUS

Of the 221 brothels licensed by the Parisian authorities in 1930, nearly 90% were small-time operations with fewer than two dozen employees and single-family staffs. In the guidebooks, they were usually listed as *maisons de rendez-vous* ("Houses of Contact") or *maisons de passé* ("Houses of Call"). The terms first appeared in 1900 and, after three decades, were constantly retitled in a puzzling assortment of coded categories. Unlike the *maisons de tolérance,* many of the two-story brothels flaunted unified motifs or decorated quarters devoted to solitary locales, like Shanghai, Rome, Naples, or Northern India. Yet even these environments were patently ersatz. For instance, *Aux Belles Japonaises*, despite its name, had no

OPPOSITE: Léo Fontan, *Le Sphinx*, 1933

ABOVE: Brodsky, *Aux Belles Japonaises*, 1935

BELOW: Customer at the *Antinéa*, 1936

TOP: Gustave Assire, *The Selection* (1926)

BOTTOM: Charles Laborde, *The Parade* (1930)

OPPOSITE: A *Tableau Vivant*, circa 1930

FOLLOWING: Selection Album from *Chez Iris*, 1929

Japanese girls and its house song that the proprietor banged out on an upright piano was "Nights of China; Warm, Snuggly Nights."

Most of the *maisons de rendez-vous* were storefront neighborhood joints that required little advertising or promotional schemes. The clientele consisted of walk-in regulars, who worked or lived nearby, and their after-hours companions. Customers generally drank, blathered about their daily routines, or repeated the latest tabloid gossip before initiating any sexual activity. For the men, hired ladies, and entrepreneurs, the social setting deliberately emulated the fixed contours of bourgeois domesticity with a slightly more upbeat finale.

The larger *maisons de rendez-vous* eschewed the everyday familiarities, replacing them with upscale boutique-like service. *Sous-maîtresses*, or occasionally the madams themselves, brought out oversized photo albums of the prostitutes with the relevant information (age, place of birth, and so forth) scribbled on the edges of the snapshots.

More intimate venues beckoned the *filles de maison* into the foyer or parlor, where a solitary customer personally inspected the available merchandise. The light-hearted negotiation, parade, appraisal, and selection process magnified the erotic hierarchy for the middle-class consumer. During the ten-minute transaction, he was no longer some desperate John but a modern-day pasha.

Instead of parades, some *maisons* staged miniature music-hall displays for groups of clients, called *tableaux vivants* or *scènes lubriques*. These amateur theatricals often involved live or recorded songs, nominal set pieces, stage lighting, and short scenarios. Typically the girls appeared in extremely provocative costumes and enacted blithe pornographic sketches. Although the plots varied from S&M dumb shows to scripted one-acts, all of them shared one homogeneous feature: at some point in the action, both the dominant and submissive participants revealed their bare buttocks.

Mlle Suzanne 18 ans
Miss Venus 1929

Mlle Germaine 20 ans
Steno - Dactylo

Miss Severa 28 ans

Mlle Dolores 24 ans
de Marseille

! Dodo ! 13 ans.
en présence de sa tante
seulement X

Mlle Odette 23 ans
Fausse maigre

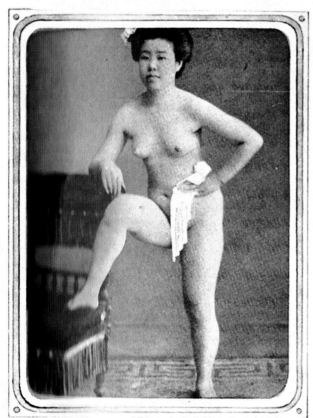

Mlle Kamisasaki
pensionnaire de Yoshiwara

Madame H..B
Femme du monde   seulement sur
rendez-vous !!

ABOVE LEFT: Theo King, *Foyer of a Sado-Masochistic Brothel,* 1932

ABOVE RIGHT: Germaine Hirschefeld, Torture Chamber in the *Temple de Vénus,* 1934

Frenchmen traditionally assessed the gynecological health of prostitutes through a fastidious, if quick, study of their unadorned derrières. A smooth, unblemished backside indicated both youthful vigor and venereal well-being. Curiously, the madams and the girls themselves obsessed over the shape, muscular plasticity, firmness, and tissue density of the breasts. Radiant skin tones between the shoulders and stomach, upright nipples, and a balanced configuration received delighted accolades from the *sous-maîtresses* and their assistants. *Vive la différence!*

Although the majority of the *maisons de tolérance* reserved at least one basement room for torture or flagellation scenes, these chambers were largely ornamental and considered bogus arenas for the infliction of pain and erotic punishment. The prerequisite chains and cuffs almost always consisted of comfortable replicas and blood was seldom drawn. The masked *femmes*, while engagingly attired, could not be considered to be experienced dominas. Their roles were obviously faked in these lively sessions.

The true "Black Rooms" or "Houses of Torture" could be found in specialized *maisons de rendez-vous.* Altogether there were about fifteen of these authentic S&M brothels in Paris. In the tarted-up medieval dungeons, the whips, *martinets,* and implements of physical agony were real and the girls genuine enthusiasts of sadistic pleasure. For the most part, the "Houses of Shudders" appealed to free-spending foreigners. Pidgin German was the second language of exchange.

Marie-Thérèse Cointré, whose 1946 memoir *The Life of a Prostitute* was serialized in Jean-Paul Sartre's *Les Temps modernes,* recorded one such encounter in a backroom of a République café:

Most of the customers were weird little guys. I came back lots of times with one who made me shit on his chest: then he'd lick my ass clean. Monsieur got that treatment for a hundred *francs* a slice. There was another one who made me stick a pin into the tips of his tits and burn them with a cigarette. Another bought me a pair of shoes: he stretched out naked on the floor and made me walk over him wearing the new shoes: he never used to come, but the exercise would get his prick up. These old fuckers don't usually don't get hard. They show up just to give their eyes a thrill.

Brothels for women (or *maisons des hommes*) proved to be another winning tourist attraction although the comic folklore that they generated outlasted their heyday. Each of the three unlicensed houses provided sporadic employment for would-be Parisian gigolos and stranded artists down on their luck. In the main, the clientele were well-to-do American or British housewives. Some liberated types merely sought to imitate the nocturnal pursuits of their husbands and fathers. After all, the emancipated ladies were temporarily domiciled in the City of Love. Others appeared so needy or attention-starved that they arrived in pairs for a discreet afternoon dalliance or an evening of narcissistic lovemaking.

The male *maisons à estaminet* (also known as "Houses of Assignment") were installed in the mid-twenties and then forcibly closed by the *police des mœurs* in 1932. The women who ran them did not bother to legally register their businesses and publicized their services only through word-of-mouth. Beginning in 1928, the popular newsweeklies had a field day exposing these "Houses of Flattery" as synthetic emporiums for shy Anglo-Saxon matrons, deluded flirts, or Francophilic dick-hounds.

LEFT: Walter Plantikow, *The Selection*, 1926

RIGHT: Ferdinand Kóra, *The Parade at Chez Godenot*, 1928

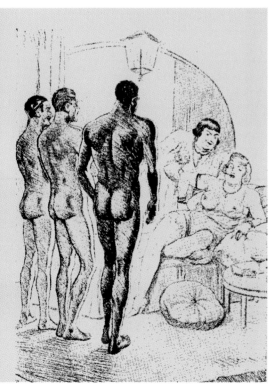

ABOVE: Jules Pascin, *The Temple de Sappho*, 1928

The most highly regarded of the *maisons des hommes* was *Chez Ann*. It was located in a four-story building with an enclosed courtyard near the Étoile. The ambiance there matched the chi-chi neighborhood; Chez Ann shimmered with bourgeois refinement, diplomatic subtly, and winking deceit. Everything was ceremonious and indirect. Both the *danseurs de madame* and women behaved as if they were conducting a nonmonetary social transaction.

The dowager-dressed madam presented the rent-boys as authentic "Russian nobles." At least one-half of the Slavic "princes" were, in fact, gay dandies from Montmartre. If addressed in Russian, they were instructed to respond with tight-lipped shrugs and an eye-rolling sigh. In the middle of tea or dinner, the female customers were encouraged to choose the object of their affection. The couples then moved to a separate salon and finally to a second-floor chamber. The street-smart Lotharios serviced between five to eight ladies each eight-hour session. (Most were delighted to receive the standard daily fee of two hundred *francs*, exactly 30% of the house charge.)

Chez Godenot on Rue Blanche attracted a more predatory tryster. The overall environment discouraged romantic pretense or the fineries of elegant seduction; rapacious coupling was the norm. Female clients expected caressing pleasures without any obligation to reciprocate. Even the gramophone speakers in the plush bedrooms were set on full volume to prevent unnecessary small talk. Madame Godenot's *danseurs* knew that they were paid orgasm specialists, pickup vassals, and not misplaced aristocrats hired to while away a dreamy-eyed and amorous evening.

Another bordello in the 2nd *Arrondissement* was celebrated as the *point d'attraction* for the indigenous lesbian set. This was the *Temple de Sappho*. Like other houses of assignment, it functioned as meeting space for the procurement of *filles de maison* but here both the buyers and the merchandise were of the same gentler sex.

The prepubescent Sappho girls and their more mature teammates were brought out from behind ceiling-to-floor curtains and then pushed into the dance floor for a quick tango or some teasing display of affection. The older prostitutes were notoriously pushy and usually rushed the negotiations. "Should we get married tonight?" was their routine come-on. Most didn't even bother to give their Christian names. After one of the *maîtresses* financially sealed the arrangement, the randy patron and her charge were directed to a nearby hotel, where their deviant escapade could swiftly commence.

MAISONS D'ABATTAGE

Maisons d'abattage, or "Slaughter Houses," referred to the lowest-grade and cheapest brothels. Here the commercial pairing of sex partners and their fleshly consummation was hideously engineered. (Only the hygienic conditions defied any industrial standards.) Yet the Slaughter Houses had their devotees and considerable

fan base. Typical clients included blue-collar wage-earners; Arab, North African, and Asian conscript laborers from France's expansive Empire; and servicemen on leave. For this outlier audience, mechanical, cursory, and thrifty sex was the draw. By 1938, twelve *maisons d'abattage* were officially recognized by vice police.

Fort Monjol was widely considered the nadir of the Slaughter Houses. This somber place in Belleville exuded evil and "sinister beauty." It was the last stop for prostitutes before their earthly demise. Many of them had been summarily dismissed from other *maisons closes* or condemned as unsightly lepers.

In November 1926, this "cemetery of love" was finally condemned and demolished. Most of the miserable girls migrated to the Rue de la Charbonnière, where they diligently patrolled the embankments of that mean street.

LEFT: Dri, *The Doorway*, 1931

TOP RIGHT: Eugène Atget, *Fort Monjol*, 1924

BOTTOM RIGHT: *Paris Sex-Appeal* (May 1934)

The cheapest and the least problematic of the *maisons d'abattage* was the *Moulin Galant*, commonly known as the *Fourcy*, the "10," or *Fourcaga*. (Sometimes it was advertised as "*Chez Paulette*.") In the parlor, one could detect just the scents of a Maghreb *souk*, antiseptic, and cheap perfume.

All couplings were pretty much random, according to the *visiteur* and prostitute's place in the two opposing lines in the hallway. The take-it-in-stride girls usually accommodated twenty to thirty clients each night. Their normal hours were 2 a.m. to 2 p.m. The tariff here (in 1929) was 5.25 *francs*, which was divided between the *fille* (2.50 *francs*), the house (2.50 *francs*), and twenty-five centimes for a fresh towel. The first-floor rooms were totally obscured with tobacco fumes.

Le Panier Fleuri was a bit of the Casbah in the 18th *Arrondissement*. Its slogan was "Five *francs* for five minutes: room, towel, and lady included." The clientele were *Sidis* (immigrant laborers from the North African colonies), off-duty sailors, fishmongers, and the unemployed.

In the huge Selection Room, the customers were directed to a wall, like convicts, and told to choose one of the girls who paraded in front of them. Everyone was addressed as a number.

The forty hard-faced and chunky "nymphs" were outfitted in short, flimsy slips that facilitated quick encounters. A few girls were crippled or obviously pregnant. Each turned an average of sixty tricks on Saturdays, Sundays, and holidays. Some of the *trottoirs* were so skilled and the patrons so horny that ejaculation would occur before any intercourse.

On the two upper levels were twenty compartments that resembled prison cells. Every room had a filthy mattress on the floor, next to a washbasin, and a musty rag hanging from the wall. The proprietor, Maurice le Croquemort, who made a small fortune from this enterprise, formerly ran a funeral parlor. ✤

LEFT: Marcel Vertès, *The Selection*, 1926

STAGING PARIS

CHAPTER 5

P ARIS WAS NOT THE ONLY CITY in Europe that was known for its lax morals and wholesale traffic in sexual merchandise. During the 1920s, Berlin, Hamburg, and, to a lesser extent, Barcelona acquired international reputations for their expansive red-light districts and other unregulated sites of carnal pleasure. In France alone, however, eroticism and nudity achieved a prominence, a coveted place in its most elevated artistic venues.

Parisian revue houses and nightspots during the interwar period relentlessly traded in naked displays. And these raffish offerings were inescapable to the general public. Scenes of nude female bodies in stylish repose were photographically captured in the color centerfolds of the metropolis entertainment monthlies.

OPPOSITE: Brassaï, *Dancer Gisèle at the* Boule Blanche, 1932

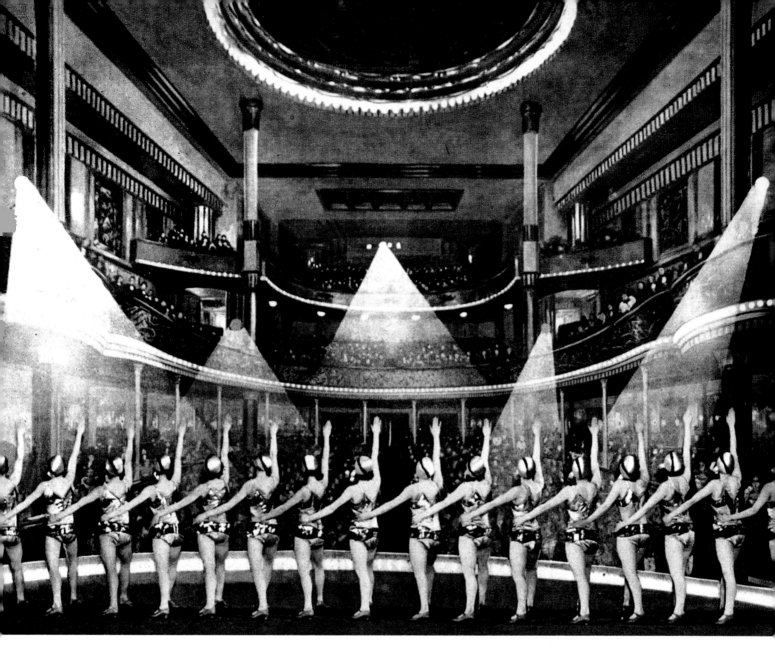

ABOVE: Folies Bergère, The Alfred Jackson Stars in *The Folies' Factory,* 1931

What was hidden, surreptitious, markedly underground, or ephemeral in most other cities became pivotal to Paris' identity: the theatricalization of sex.

Inside the dozens of music-hall and nightclub prosceniums, embroidered licentious fantasies found their extravagant realization. Gaudy exhibitions of powdered flesh here were not gratuitous add-ons to the productions. From curtain rise to curtain call, they were the chief attraction. Individual stars with huge fan bases, like Mistinguett and Maurice Chevalier, did emerge from these erotic emporiums yet the featured celebrities had to integrate their singing, choreographic, athletic, or comic skills with the high-kicking synchronized *figurantes*.

In the like-minded variety houses of Berlin, London, and New York, a tuxedoed and super-animated M.C. usually guided the show's progress, introducing the acts, cueing the orchestra, and providing humorous commentary. Yet Parisian revues rarely employed *conférenciers*. The unerring French producers were fearless in this regard. The onslaught of milky-skinned *nues* and dazzling set pieces were normally sufficient eye candy to keep the city's nocturnal voyeurs thoroughly engaged.

MUSIC-HALLS

The first major music-halls in Paris, the *Folies Bergère* and *Moulin Rouge*, opened to great fanfare in the 1870s and 1880s. The image-packed posters promised spectacular divertissements involving the latest popular dances, pantomime, circus acrobatics, provocative ballet sketches, P.T. Barnum-like freak shows, comic monologists, *Opéra bouffe*, and a flashy assortment of foreign vaudeville routines. Jolted by the cascade of encouraging reviews, *Belle Époque* audiences flocked to the former Pigalle dance halls.

By the turn of the century, the Montmartre variety houses altered their municipal billings. They began to promote a less globally diverse and more indigenous menu of attractions. "The temples of sensation" suddenly jettisoned the stupefying and eccentric acts from abroad; their new performances exploded with visions of an urbane Paris. Overnight, revue entrepreneurs replaced the shopworn itinerant routines with local *chanteuses* and erotic novelty pageants. Journalists quickly endorsed the reconfigured programs as authentic expressions

ABOVE: Georges Villa, *Casino de Paris: Paris in Festival*, 1929

of *la Ville-Lumière* — the contemporary music-halls had transformed themselves into "cathedrals of women."

LES FOLIES BERGÈRE

Since its inception in 1871, the Folies Bergère underwent a radical reinvention every ten or fifteen years but its most celebrated incarnation began in 1918, when Paul Derval (1880–1966) took charge of its annual productions. Under his discerning management, the Folies doubled in size, which his agents quickly billed as "the most renowned music-hall in the world." Most tourists deemed it to be France's national theatre.

The riotous, eye-popping, head-pounding revues were mainly recognized for their visual splendor and scenic investitures that included waterfalls, chariot arenas, and urban roadways. Russian-born Erté created many of the breathtaking sets and costuming. In fact, there were so many scene shifts that spectators often experienced vertiginous headaches and complained about them in the tourist guidebooks. Teams of British showgirls, like the Alfred Jackson Stars and Laurence Tiller Girls, executed most of the glitzy precision work. The individual dancers or duets rarely startled but the budget-shattering numbers always concluded in sexy Gallic *tableaux vivants*.

Derval drilled his choruses like cadres of volunteers for a peacetime Bastille Day parade. Unfortunately, the backstage haste during the fast-draw scenic changes could not always be cloaked: the naked showgirls habitually appeared in faulty makeup (smeared purple eyelids, lashes plastered with mascara, cheeks painted yellow and rouged on top). In picture-perfect form or not, they portrayed every kind of wine, *apéritif*, tree creature, marine animal, or archaic occupation, like Egyptian priestess, Roman gladiator, and Renaissance courtier. More than one-third of any production was devoted to them. In 1937, Derval defended his barrage of autonomous *figurantes* to his influential cultural critics, "Ah, these nude women, if I got rid of them, I would have to close up shop."

Outside the theatre, a quagmire of taxi cabs, limos, and ticket-holders signaled the season's premiere. Near the front box office, old men hawked the latest *derty-picure* booklets from nearby Pigalle. Inside, well-coiffed matrons tendered similar risqué items to curious couples and non-French speakers.

The Folies' mammoth promenade-lobby was as large as the theatre itself, with five bars scattered around the walls with scores of circular marble-topped tables and small gilded chairs. In the center was a fountain surrounded by palms. Gilded stairways led upward to an erotic sideshow, the *Danse de Ventre*. Around a swaying coal-black, seven-foot wooden figure, four African women enacted a primitive naked rite. There was also a shooting gallery, where one could fire at bottles with 22mm rifles.

By the WCs and in the foyer, several dozen predatory *femmes* — including shockingly unattractive ones — offered their wares to any standalone males. Champagne cocktails were available at the American bar; there were also separate booths for the purchase of beribboned cartons or tins of chocolates (twenty *francs*, *merci*), cigarettes, and perfume. Roving *cocottes* and *mannequins* frequently cajoled these packaged treasures from seated tourists. The girls normally resold the unopened parcels back to the vendors for half-price after the grand finale.

The Folies' clientele consisted of flush sightseers and tired French businessmen. U.S. Army guidebooks in 1946 maintained that more than sixty million spectators had been "fleeced" by Derval since the Armistice. (There was no need to know French in order to follow the vapid stage dialogue. In fact, linguistic ignorance was thought to be a singular advantage.)

Despite the occasional public outcry, the Folies Bergère had so successfully marketed itself as a must-see tourist draw that the sex-kitsch amusement venue never closed or scheduled a dark night.

LEFT: Folies Bergère, *Plain Folies*, 1923

RIGHT: Folies Bergère, *A Breeze of Folie*, 1927

A FOLIES' SMASH PROGRAM (1930)

A SUPERSPECTACLE IN 60 SENSATIONS

FIRST ACT

THE SINS OF PARIS
1. PARIS, THE CITY OF JOY
2. THE DRUNKEN CHARM OF PARIS
3. LUXURIOUS PARIS
4. VOLUPTUOUS PARIS
5. GAY PARIS

BALLET OF THE FAUNES

PULCINELLOS!
1. A BABY'S PULCINELLO
2. THE LIFE OF A PULCINELLO
3. THE PULCINELLOS IN A DRAWER

IN THE SOUK
1. THE BAZAAR STREET
2. SMOKE FROM THE HOOKAH

A STRIKE OF RATTLESNAKES

ONLY A LITTLE WORD

A QUEEN IN FOLIE (Imperial Russia's Catherine the Great)
WEEKEND
1. AN ENGLISHMAN IN PARIS
2. A FRENCHMAN IN LONDON

WHEN THE BANJOS PLAY

50TH ANNIVERSARY OF THE FOLIES-BERGÈRE
1. THE FOLIES-BERGÈRE IN 1880
2. A REVUE FROM THE FOL'-BERG' IN 1900
3. A PATRIOTIC TABLEAU IN 1918
4. THE FOLIES-BERGÈRE FINALE IN 1930 (Paris' Colonial Exhibition)

FOLIES
BERGÈRE

1930
HUITIÈME ALBUM

A FOLIES' SMASH PROGRAM (1930)

A SUPERSPECTACLE IN 60 SENSATIONS

SECOND ACT

NAKED PARIS!
1. PARIS NUDITY
2. THE NAUGHTY NUDE
3. THE NAÏVE NUDE
4. THE WORLDLY NUDE
5. THE VEILED NUDE
6. THE CURLY NUDE
7. THE WEDDING NUDE
8. THE SUGGESTIVE NUDE
9. THE EXOTIC NUDE
10. THE LASCIVIOUS NUDE
11. THE EROTIC NUDE
12. THE SADISTIC NUDE

PSYCHOANALYSIS OF EUROPEANS BY AN AMERICAN REPORTER

THE SPIRIT OF THE STAIRCASE
1. THE FIREBIRD
2. THE SPANISH CABARET

JAZZ-SINGER AND DANCER

THE CELEBRATED CHIN-CHIN GIRLS

THE SIRENS OF CEYLON
1. THROUGH A PORTHOLE
2. SUBMARINE PAGEANT
3. PEARLDIVERS
4. THE RAPTURE
5. THE RIDE OF THE SIRENS

I KNOW WHAT YOU NEED

CIRCUS IMPRESSIONS

AMERICAN REPORTER: "What is your favorite activity?"
FRENCHMAN: "Les petites poules!" ["Chicks!"]
AMERICAN: "Oh, an amateur bird watcher!"
ENGLISHMAN: "We like to down the hatch!"
AMERICAN: "Oh, pet hobby: getting cock-eyed!"

AMERICAN REPORTER: "What is your favorite activity?"
GERMAN: "Making babies!"
AMERICAN: "Oh, be fruitful and multiply!"
ITALIAN: "To assassinate!"
AMERICAN: "Oh, pet hobby: murder!"

97. Moulin Rouge, Paris

THE MOULIN ROUGE MUSIC-HALL

ABOVE LEFT: Moulin Rouge, *La Revue Mistinguett* (*La Rampe*, 1925)

ABOVE RIGHT: Stereoscopic Card of the *Moulin Rouge*, 1907

BELOW: Moulin Rouge, *Better than Nude: "Birds of Paradise,"* 1925

OPPOSITE: Léon Bonnotte, *Moulin Rouge Night*, 1925

Beginning in 1889, the *Moulin Rouge* on the Boulevard de Clichy, with its red windmill tower and lattice sails, established itself as the hub of Montmartre nightlife. The emblematic framework secured to the cabaret roof never ceased to rotate. In its first incarnation, the *fin-de-siècle* dance hall and pleasure garden was made famous by the arresting Japanese woodcut-like posters that the dwarf painter Henri Toulouse-Lautrec had created for the institution. His Impressionist canvases of twirling cancan dancers, tables of hollow-eyed absinthe devotees, and flame-haired prostitutes were instantly recognizable and mounted on the walls of the adjoining Bal du Moulin Rouge.

From 1903 until its fiery destruction in 1915, the Moulin Rouge competed with the Folies Bergère as Paris' primary music-hall destination. Famous for its

multistoried sets with a mix of artistic and foreign dance attractions, its stylish shows were fast-paced, frequently included audience participation (i.e., a Prettiest Legs contest, the most inventive Cake Walk match), and ran into the early morning hours. Along with the Eiffel Tower, graphic depictions of the thatched red mill conjured up the image of only one sophisticated European city.

When the Moulin Rouge Music-Hall reopened in 1925, it was widely proclaimed as the future "House of Mistinguett," although the bubbly *chanteuse* gave no intention of settling into a solitary fixed abode. The seemingly promiscuous and long-stemmed Mistinguett (1875–1956) had already promoted herself as the avatar of Parisienne sexuality and claimed to be the highest-paid female entertainer of any nation. (Six years earlier at the *Casino de Paris*, her manager insured Miss' silk-stockinged gams for a phenomenal 500,000 *francs*.)

Starting out as a small-town flower-seller in a local restaurant, the unaging and temperamental La Miss scaled the rungs of music-hall notoriety before the Great War, brandishing a singular risqué wit and dogged showmanship. Her ability to ferret out a choice repertoire and dramatic zest disguised her untrained and tinny voice. She played guttersnipe *gamines*; love-smitten *gigolettes*, who were flung across the stage by dance partners (dolled up as Apache *mecs*); and ludicrously adorned *mannequins*, covered in columns of feathers, rhinestones, stoles, and strings of flowers. Rodin so admired Mistinguett's legs that he spoke of sculpting them as the erotic logo of French music-hall.

La Miss' liberated attitude and flamboyant theatricality — as well as her maniacal self-absorption — captivated the French public for more than five decades. With her much younger protégé (and kept lover), Maurice Chevalier, Mistinguett radiated an unrelenting sunny disposition that artfully cloaked her hardscrabble origins and lower-middle-class anxieties.

The new Moulin was indeed a marvel. Its main stage was designed according to the most opulently Art Deco specifications and equipped with the latest mechanical devices. Parisians, in general, found the revue auditorium, which seated 1500, gaudy and

AU MOULIN-ROUGE MUSIC HALL

ABOVE LEFT: *Moulin Rouge Music-Hall, Paris Revolves,* 1928

ABOVE RIGHT: Georges Léonnec, *Moulin Rouge: That's Paris!,* 1927

overdone, but its huge promenoir was open until four in the morning and accommodated another two thousand dressed-to-the-nines upper sets.

In the summer, the retractable ceiling revealed the nighttime sky of Pigalle. The intimate stage in the Roof Garden was reserved for performances during the Moulin's *fêtes de nuit*. There was also a private "Oriental Palace of Dance" sideshow, where three belly dancers in harem trousers performed a *danse du ventre*.

There were several places to eat and drink at the Moulin before, between, and after the productions: in the Roof Garden (specialty drink *cognac chéri*) and in a separate restaurant-cabaret off the foyer. A jazz band played in the outer hall through the intermissions, precluding the need for any non-corporal small talk. And during the gala suppers that followed the stage shows, costumed Moulin *artistes* did their star turns as they mingled and tangoed with the guests.

The Moulin Rouge Music-Hall extravaganzas featured pantomime ballets, more provocative *quadrilles excentriques*, twin-sister acts, historical sketches, and daredevil acrobats. The line-chorus' meticulous discipline and plastic beauty quickly became the talk of the town. At the fall premieres, fashionista couples were ushered directly from their limousines into partitioned VIP lounges by smartly attired doormen; later in the season, ticket-buyers came mostly from "the tourist class" (the dominant faction being randy Brits).

For five spectacular years, the Moulin Rouge revues elevated live nude displays and Miss' sentimental ballads to their most *charmant* and ironic heights. Yet, it was the first Parisian music-hall to fall victim to the changing social and economical conditions that upended Jazz Age extravagance, which it helped define. After the Wall Street Crash, the Moulin's interiors were gutted and converted into an unwieldy cinema that featured the variety theatre's most loathsome competition: around-the-clock projections of all-singing, all-dancing motion pictures.

CASINO DE PARIS

The *Casino de Paris* was the third largest music-hall in Paris and the one that attracted the greatest number of Frenchmen. Like the Moulin Rouge, the Casino resembled New York's Ziegfeld Follies in format and style; it also imported many Broadway and Harlem offerings, like the Black Bottom, Shimmy, Lindy Hop, and Cotton Club music. It was, to be sure, America's most glamorous show biz outpost in interwar Montmartre. (The French performers ultimately rebelled against the salary disparities: the hard-working foreigners received salaries more than double those of their slacker counterparts.)

The Casino's producers, which usually included an American or British interloper, achieved something altogether magical and commercially inventive: their movie-paced performances generated divergent voyeuristic impressions on the foreign and French spectators. It was as if the out-of-towners and Parisian socialites had sat through two entirely different evenings.

For tourists, the Casino revues delivered on the pledge of "the raw, the risqué, and the resplendent!" The mobile staircases and sparkling backdrops nearly disappeared from view when synchronized teams of top-hatted, slender *figurines* pranced before them. Guidebooks described the early revues as "fever dreams" of "unlimited nudity" and "creamy flesh." According to *Fodor's*, the Casino de Paris was no less than "a dazzling Niagara of eroticism."

If one inquired at the concierge desks of the grand hotels, every frisky check-in would be informed that the Alfred Jackson Girls and Boys, the "Four Stars of the Tabarin," the Lawrence Tiller Girls, the "16 Red and Blond Greasley Beauties" and all the cutesy-nudie sister acts were the Casino's not-to-be-missed featured delights.

ABOVE LEFT: Casino de Paris, *Loves of Paris* Playbill, 1938

ABOVE RIGHT: Léon Bonnotte, *The Eight Exciting Skibine Ladies*, 1927

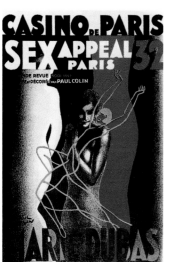

Yet the legitimate French press rendered these girl groups scant notice. Parisians adored the Casino revues for a more lofty reason: they revealed the secret history of their seductive metropolis — it was a vast urban labyrinth of pancaked temptation and tenacious erotic pitfalls.

The annual revue titles practically gave away the game. Beginning with its restoration in 1924, most of the Casino productions invoked the city's name in thick banners of marquee lights: *Bonjour Paris* (1924), *Paris in Flowers* (1925), *Revue Paris* (1926), *Paris* (1927), *The Wings of Paris* (1928), *Paris, You Charm* (1929), *Paris Miss* (1929), *Paris Moves* (1930), *Paris Shines* (1931), *Sex-Appeal Paris-32* (1932), *Joy of Paris* (1932), *Vive Paris* (1933), *Pleasures of Paris* (1936), *You Sing, Paris* (1936), *Paris From Joy* (1937), *Paris Jazz* (1938), *Spectacle of Paris* (1938), *Loves of Paris* (1939), *Paris-London* (1939), *To You Paris* (1942), and *Charming Paris* (1945). Like the ubiquitous pop *chansons* that were pumped out of Left Bank bistros, they heralded Paname's witchy allure.

Each of the Casino's comic (and occasionally downbeat) skits was story-driven, usually involving the star or star-couples' hanky-panky dilemma. The sumptuous naked ballets, color-saturated revolving sets, and Tin Pan Alley-like orchestrations surfaced as mere filler for sexual problem-solving. In the Casino's knotty ethos, Pigalle tramps, women of the world, music-hall *nues*, coquettish schoolgirls, and veiled concubines proved to be universal stumbling blocks to familial sobriety. An exonerative Paris, though, in the curtain-rising finale, inevitably parted its bejeweled arms to embrace the world's errant playboys and playgirls.

No one characterized the Suffering Young Man more unconvincingly than Maurice Chevalier (1888–1972). La Miss discovered the fifteen-year-old scamp at a low Parisian dive and transformed him into a dandy sensation. (She was his senior by thirteen years.) The straw-hatted *chanteur* made his fortune at the

Casino and within a few seasons acquired the appellation "Monsieur Paris."

The one music-haller to achieve international standing, the debonair Chevalier rode the crosscurrents of the world variety stage as it boomeranged into the new sound media. In part, this was due to his fluency in English, which he picked up in a German POW camp from a fellow British inmate. (In the midst of the Great War, Miss persuaded her bosom admirer Alfonso XIII, the King of Spain, to petition the Kaiser for Chevalier's release. It was the only recorded example of an Imperial German repatriation based on a three-way.)

Chevalier's carefree gigolo persona inspired composer-and-lyricist teams in Paris, London, Broadway, and Hollywood. It was an intriguingly fresh archetype — the innocuous, *bon vivant* alley-cat. In 1930, he received Academy Award nominations for Best Actor in two Paramount musicals and in 1959 accepted the Honorary Oscar for "Contributions to the World of Entertainment for More than a Half Century."

Yet behind Chevalier's soft-shoeing "every little breeze" outlook was a noxious emotional core, animated by memories of abandonment, suppressed homosexual desire, malicious Francophilia, paranoia, and class envy. The embittered *boulevardier*, like Miss, was berated for his obsessive penny-pinching and even negotiated an insurance policy in Hollywood that duly compensated him if he ever lost his Gallic accent. Chevalier's postwar infatuation with Communism, which placed him on the State Department's blacklist, baffled everyone, especially his Hollywood paramours.

OPPOSITE TOP: Casino de Paris, *Parade of France: Arabelle and Her Partners*, 1934

OPPOSITE MIDDLE: *Paris Miss* Poster, 1929

OPPOSITE BOTTOM: *Sex-Appeal Paris-32* Poster, 1932

ABOVE: Casino de Paris, *Paris*, "Symphony in Purple," 1927

LEFT: Maurice Chevalier in *Paris*, "Path of My Heart," 1927

With his star turn in Vincent Minnelli's 1958 lush MGM romance *Gigi*, all references to Chevalier's wartime collaboration during the Occupation and anti-Americanism were expediently dropped. The Monsieur Paris mimic, in the end, was true to his namesake.

In the mid-twenties, two American solo entertainers, Barbette and Joséphine Baker, mesmerized Parisian audiences with their erotic novelty numbers and iconoclastic lifestyles. Both were second-tier, eccentric performers on the New York stage but overnight bolted to Continental music-hall stardom. Championed by mainstream French reviewers and their avant-garde opposition, the two outlandish loners received a stupendous welcome in their soon to be adopted home city, a reception that was, naturally, unfathomable in the land of their birth. Barbette and Baker were immortalized as Casino regulars.

Vander Clyde (1898–1973) began his career as a high-wire and trapeze artist on the Midwest vaudeville circuit. The Flying Alfaretto Sisters hired the Texas-born acrobat as a male replacement for their deceased sibling. One night, against their wishes, Clyde donned one of the Alfarettos' sequined tutus and went on as Barbette, their lost sister. It was an unalloyed triumph.

In an inspired moment, Clyde meshed perilous circus derring-do with gender impersonation. Curiously, he always claimed otherwise. Over decades of reporters' inquiries, the famed aerialist and cross-dresser asserted that his spectacular presentations were the product of an ineffable corporal possession. A phantom creature, which Clyde christened Barbette, mysteriously entered his body before every performance. He maintained that Barbette was an actual life form with her own thoughts, flirtatious style, and big-top skills. The flat-chested and small-hipped enigmatic figure defied sexual boundaries, being neither woman nor man. The spell of Barbette enveloped Clyde in the green room, as he worked the trapeze bars, and long after he took his thunderous curtain calls. Barbette faded away with the night but only in hesitant waves.

At the Casino de Paris, Barbette first appeared as an attractive young woman in a silvery-gold wig and trailing silver lamé dress. She negotiated a long tightrope, executed a series of aerial leaps from hand-rings to stirrups, and then wowed 'em with her rude female-to-male unveiling when Clyde stepped out of his silken costume and pulled off his wig. It was the strangest and most persuasive transvestite act Paris had ever witnessed. Jean Cocteau extolled the *artiste* as a wonder who was above "incongruity, death, bad taste, indecency, indignation." Igor Stravinsky favorably compared Barbette's feminine shrugs and soaring dives to Nijinsky's nimble pirouettes and gravity-defying *jetés*.

Despite the collective raves, misfortune and tragedy weighed down Barbette's towering feats. Suitors of both sexes and all orientations doggedly pursued him. Closeted transvestites from France's industrial elite, lesbian lion tamers, Sorbonne professors, and otherwise straight business types waited impatiently in the Casino's backrooms, cradling vases of rose bouquets or boxed diamond engagement rings. Many thwarted lovers disrupted Barbette's act with plaintive cries or violent outbursts in the auditorium. Others wrote sick love letters threatening suicide.

(A few even made good on their declarations.) In 1934, one week before the Night of the Long Knives and his assassination by the SS, the Nazi chieftain and open pedophile Ernst Roehm penned an invitation to Barbette, "You are more than beautiful. I love you. I must see you immediately."

Two years later, Clyde returned to New York City, where he performed as Barbette but for only one evening. After the ten o'clock show in a Times Square theatre, he came down with a painful bout of chills and a physician was rushed to his hotel. Clyde had contracted a disease, something medically unknown, which paralyzed his entire body. The variety headliner was unable to stand upright or walk for nearly two years. Convalescing back in Texas, he wrote his fans that Barbette had died during an emergency transfusion in a Manhattan hospital.

Shortly after 1940, the wizard of gender mystification and sexual illusion started a career as an aerial trainer and big-top director. His specialty was female aerialist teams. Clyde worked as an advisor in Hollywood and Broadway until his death in 1973 from an overdose of pills.

ABOVE: Baker and Chiquita (*Le Sourire*, 1933)

RIGHT: Casino de Paris, *Joy of Paris* Poster, 1932

Joséphine Baker (1906–1975) was yet another transatlantic concoction. Engaged as the eccentric female lead in 1925 for a thinly conceived Afro-American variety show, *La Revue Nègre*, Baker mugged her way into the entertainment columns of the French press. Within one year, the intuitive but untrained performer catapulted into the upper stratospheres of Parisian music-hall and French society. She became the talk of the city and would remain so for exactly one half-century.

Within the confines of Broadway's black revues, the teenage Josephine was a minor chorus-girl standout. Her putty-kneed and cross-eyed renditions of the Charleston registered as bizarre parodies of the current dance craze. In fact, the limber dancer's wacky solos were considered amusing and proper punctuation for a string of not-so-serious colored musicals. The impossibly sleek Joe-Josephine, with her plastered-down hair and quivery legs, was billed as America's "coon" Chaplin.

In Paris, *la Baker* assumed a different character. She embodied the competing visions of contemporary Negritude — the dusky carefree princess from pre-Christian, tribal Africa and the sophisticated *hotsa* dancer, who greeted millionaires in anything-goes Harlem nightclubs. Baker's lacquered nudity, at home and onstage, projected a doubled aura of primitive sexuality and its modern Parisian equivalent.

Starting at the Folies Bergère and then at the Casino, Joséphine appeared topless in a series of comical jungle sketches. Belts of phallic bananas or ridiculously tiny palm leaves covered her genitals. And wild animals, especially her pet cheetah, Chiquita, pranced around her as the "Black Pearl" warbled through her signature *chansons* such as "I Have Two Loves." (Backstage, the ever jealous Miss referred to Baker as "that disgusting monkey.")

Functionally illiterate, Joséphine couldn't even sign her own autographs without assistance from bodyguards or well-wishers. Nonetheless, *Bakermania* had firmly planted itself in Paris. La Baker porcelain dolls, waist-dangling pearl necklaces, artificial hairpieces, and patterned flapper gowns appeared in the finest shops. Fashion designers and men-about-town guided and schooled the caramel-skinned sex goddess as best they could. (She bleached her mulatto skin with lemon juice every morning.) In the forgiving minds of their clients and mates, the dashing Galahads were the urbane counterparts of white saviors or carpetbaggers who descended into the Congo basin or the antebellum plantation South for an exotic escapade.

If starring in the Casino revues was not enough, Baker married an Italian count on a whim and opened her own jazz club, *Chez Joséphine*, in Pigalle. Like everything else that "the Maple Nut Sundae" sank her giddy soul into, her diminutive *boîte* was an enormous financial success, attracting all manner of expats and first-nighters. It flourished until the German invasion.

TOP: Palace Music-Hall Boulevards, *Paris-Voyeur* Program, 1925

BOTTOM: Palace Music-Hall Boulevards, *The Palace of Nudes*, 1928

REVUE HOUSES AND NIGHTCLUBS

By the late twenties, tens of smaller revue houses and lavish nightclubs beckoned the most adventurous Parisians as they vied for the tourist dollar. Guidebooks generally listed between eighty and two hundred of these drink-yourself-silly establishments. Approximately half of them attempted to out-sex and out-provoke the big three music-halls with more markedly erotic productions, greater intimate contact with the performers, or with expansive merry-making surroundings.

For a while the *Palace Music-Hall Boulevards* was the preferred hub of the indigenous flapper set. Its elaborate revues specialized in risqué Russian and South American themes. Not only was the atmosphere at Palace outrageously pornographic, its artistic sets and costumes seemed as if they had been borrowed from the covert Montmartre studios churning out similar stuff down the street. Usually only one imported star interrupted the untamed comings and doings until another kind of scandal brought the theatre to a temporary ignominious halt.

In September 1933, Oscar Dufrenne, the Palace director and a city councilor, was found murdered in his upstairs office. The police suspected the assassin to be a male prostitute disguised as a sailor, but, according to the pulp weeklies, the masqueraded street tough was mysteriously discharged and the crime remained unsolved. The Palace was shuttered for a few days and then reopened under new management.

Another music-hall/nightclub dear to high-stepping locals, the *Concert Mayol*, assured even more daring, chic-chic, and partisan variety

ABOVE LEFT: Concert Mayol, *Oh! Nude!* Program, 1946

ABOVE RIGHT: Sem, *Lido Pool*, 1929

BELOW: *What a Beautiful Nude*, 1926

entertainment. Here, the hat-check girls, program vendors, cabaret ushers, and washroom ladies were reputed to be the most "insolent and rapacious" in Pigalle. They routinely shortchanged foreigners and turned their backs on them after pocketing the "tips."

In a typical revue, *What a Beautiful Nude* (1926), the topless *chanteuse* Ginette Delly rallied her countrymen in a denunciation of the American State Department and the crude behavior of its citizens. She began her sketch hawking nude statues of herself: "It's a good likeness, *n'est-ce pas*? Well, how much for me?" From the wings, a cast member whispered, "No, my dear Mademoiselle, you cannot complete this transaction until you have purchased a tax stamp from Finance Minister Doumer! He needs cash to pay our debt to the United States!" An outraged Delly protested, "But I have nothing! Anyone can see that! I am like France! And France has no money for such bogus charges!"

The Mayol audience seconded her objections with shrieks of "Down with *l'Oncle Sam*!" Suddenly an "American" spectator (a baggy-pants comic in horn-rimmed glasses) stepped up to the stage and announced that "the good women of France" could liquidate their national debt if they paid a sales tax for each "passionate encounter."

After slapping him across the face, Delly offered a contrary proposal: "If we are credited with three *francs* every time an American gets drunk in Paris, then the USA will immediately owe France a windfall in international fees!" This brought the audience to its feet and the naked revue commenced in a more elevated jingoist spirit.

Still more super-opulent nightclubs opened at the end of the twenties. The *Lido*, "Venice transported to Paris," had a glass-bottom platform for dancing and revues with a public swimming pool, beauty parlor, and Turkish bath (for an extra twenty and twenty-five *francs*) adjacent to the dance floor. During its first season in 1928, a tipsy and fully clothed

F. Scott Fitzgerald jumped into the main *Lido* fountain and, of course, his dutiful and equally inebriated spouse, Zelda, followed suit. Both were arrested and fined.

The *Chez les Nudistes*, known as the "Jerusalem of Pleasure," did little to disguise its cheesy appeal and had a permanent ensemble of twenty-four "Voluptuous Nude Dancers." This was the logical wrap for the high-society mob that taxied from one wild nightclub to the next. And it was the favored haunt of Argentine *bons vivants* and their mistresses. Almost all of the naked revue clubs outlasted the Depression, Occupation, and Libération under a shifting banner of freshly minted names, scam fronts, and unlikely intermediaries. ✣

ABOVE: *Chez les Nudistes: The Nude Is King*, 1934

BELOW: Teddy Piaz, *Côte d'Azur*, 1934

GAY PAREE

In Paris, receptions, parties, and five o'clock teas, given by homosexuals for homosexuals, are very popular. At almost all of them, musical performances play a large role. Some are highly aesthetic.

— Magnus Hirschfeld, *The Homosexuality of Men and Women* (Berlin: Marcus, 1919) —

For a night, one night only, these human beings reveal their true naked selves. Tomorrow, they will be unrecognizable, disguised in the masks that society's hypocrisy forces them to wear.

— Jean Laurent, "Magic City," *La Rampe* (April 1930) —

BEFORE 1905, THERE WERE FEW objective or scientifically neutral terms in French jurisprudence to describe homosexual behavior or attachments. Men and women who sought the sexual comfort and exclusive companionship with members of their own gender could not be easily classified or defined. They were branded "inverts" or outcasts with "twisted souls" — mincing pedophilic trolls, demented size queens or man-haters, even sociopathic ogres.

France's magistrates and psychologists acknowledged the existence of same-sex desire but it had been long associated with deviant nobility from the

OPPOSITE: Brassaï, *Bal du Magic City*, 1931

prerevolutionary past and their progeny, unhinged Symbolist artists, genetically inbred criminals, and, of course, lust-besotted clergymen. How could any normal Frenchman from a stable family background elect to forego blissful congress with the opposite sex or reject the biblical/national mandate to reproduce? (Religious celibates, marines and colonial troops in faraway isolation, mental degenerates, and asexual providers were the exceptions to this pressing social command.)

Public attitudes in Paris concerning the dangers of homosexuality gradually diminished in the prewar era. Yes, fairies and *tantes* could be observed in the lowest, most bestial edges of society but they also inhabited its upper spectrums as well. In fact, France's foremost writers and theatre practitioners at the turn of the century, distinguished intellects like Robert de Montesquiou, Marcel Proust, Colette, and André Gide, made no secret of their gay orientation.

Ignoring that nettlesome fact, overly effeminate male affectation and man-boy love was generally cast as "the German vice." Satirical images of Prussian officers, including the enemy's blustering General Staff, in girlish repose preceded the Great War and later evoked collective smirks when splashed across the pictorial propaganda sheets.

Beneath their spiked helmets and waxed moustaches, the Kaiser's brutes would be shown to be timid *Gretschens*. Their hyper-militancy was little more than a psychic façade constructed by a nation of pansies and baritone-voiced nancy boys. Confronted by real fighting men, the warrior descendents of ancient Galle were assured, the sissy Junker commanders and their dithering Pomeranians would break ranks and disperse in any eastward direction.

The initial advances and steadfast resolve of von Hindenburg's frontline armies between 1914 and 1918 naturally did not ameliorate France's general antipathy toward the German national character but the notion that queers-in-uniform — and, more generally, gay disposition — was tethered to cowardliness or physical debility pretty much fell out of fashion.

SOURCES OF INTERWAR QUEERDOM

Historical knowledge of Parisian gay lifestyles from the signing of the Armistice through 1946 remains imprecise, spotty, and lacking in detailed first-person documentation. Today it is difficult to get a good reading or a statistical understanding of queer Paris. There are a host of reasons for this scholarly quandary: unlike the gay men and lesbians in pre-Nazi Berlin, the aggregate of self-

— Bobette est un traître ! Il vient de se marier... avec une femme !

described homosexuals in Paris was relatively small; French culture traditionally discouraged separatist impulses and minority distinctiveness; government criminalization of homosexuality was largely ineffectual and haphazardly enforced; and, most important, no effective leadership or mass organizations emerged in the struggle for gay rights in France.

One potential spokesman, André Gide, wrote provocative homosexual fiction like the 1924 novel *Corydon*, but was condemned for defending the supremacy of pederast bonding. His cerebral militancy and unique lusts were shared by only a fraction of same-sex enthusiasts.

Overall, the queer community in France subscribed to few common goals and drifted rudderless against the hateful backlash that spewed from the reactionary and clerical opposition. (In 1920, the National Assembly passed legislation that barred the sale of condoms — those old "French letters" — and instructional pamphlets on birth control. It effectively consigned all nonbreeders into a single Francophobic bin.)

In Weimar Germany, rival homosexual publishers profitably marketed over three dozen politically based or purely hedonistic gay journals and photo-magazines. But in twentieth-century France, only one like-minded same-sex monthly appeared, *Inversions* (1924–25) and then just barely. After its fourth issue was censored, it resurfaced as *L'Amitié*.

Since sodomy was an accepted literary subject, state attorneys considered prosecuting the journal's editors on charges of pornography but that too was dropped: *Inversions* contained no sexually inflammatory passages, no illustrations, not even any personals or advertising. The dispassionate academic journal was banned on the grounds of being "anti-conception propaganda" and its directors were condemned to six months in prison.

Much of what we know about gay social life exists in the records of the *Sûreté* or in the memoirs of noteworthy Parisians. Some reporters from the weeklies *Détective Magazine* and its lesser competition *Police Magazine* wrote titillating stories about outlawed queer gatherings and their seedy venues. Oddly enough, these exposés humanized the sexual fugitives. Partly because of the travelogue

OPPOSITE TOP: Albert Guillaume, *The Judgment of Paris in Germany*, 1915

OPPOSITE MIDDLE: "Monsters and Satyrs," *L'Assiette au Beurre* (August 1903)

OPPOSITE BOTTOM: Robert Polack, *Ambiguous Couple*, 1934

TOP LEFT: "Bobette is a traitor. He just married … a woman!" *L'Assiette au Beurre* (May 1909)

TOP RIGHT: Léon Fontan, "The Action Is Not Always on the Stage," 1929

inclinations of the local publishing houses and their editors, we have a much richer accounting of Parisian gay and lesbian nightlife than the everyday interactions of typical homosexuals.

True to form, homosexual desire, "the love that dare not speak its name," was better portrayed graphically by a wide assortment of Paris' painters, cartoon illustrators, brash second-string photographers, and pornographic studios than historians using the printed word. The Hungarian photo-journalist Brassï (Gyula Halász) was, by far, the most intrepid of these dissident artists. His album *Paris de nuit* (Paris: Éditions Arts et Métiers, 1933) and magazine photographs divulged the city's secret underworlds and safeguarded them for future researchers and laymen.

GAY NIGHTLIFE

All in all, there were sixty-some "blatant" homosexual cabarets and nightspots in Paris during the twenties and thirties. The majority of these private clubs had few constraints and customers were routinely ushered in. The primary function of their doormen was more barker than storefront guardian. Just a handful of gay establishments imposed strict fraternal policies, admitting only select or vetted male patrons.

BELOW: Antonin Soungouroff, "Sodomy," 1947 (Two *Pédés*)

GLOSSARY OF HOMOSEXUAL TYPES

AMATEURS: Gay men of power and wealth.

ENTRETENEURS: Elderly queers. Always endangered by blackmailers.

FEMMES ENTRETENUES: Ladyboys. Young men who dress like girls and mimic their behavior.

FRAPPES: Gay dandies.

PÉDÉS: Pederasts. Manly queers. [Variant names: *Corydons* (from the novel by André Gide), *Pédéros* and *Pédales*.]

LAPINS ("RABBITS"): Fags. [Pejorative term.]

LOPPES: Pansies. [Old pejorative term.] [Variant name: *Lopettes*.]

MIGNONS ("Tender Ones"): Effeminate gay men. [Variant names: *Fifis*, *Invertis*, and *Lopettes*.]

PETITS JÉSUS: Lost, depraved boys between 16 and 23.

PETITS MESSIEURS: Sodomists. [Variant name: *Jésus*.]

TANTES ["AUNTIES"]: Frumpy, cross-dressing gay men. [From the German.] [Variant names: *Tatas* and *Cocottes*.]

TAPETTES: Passive homosexuals. Traditionally seeking the company of rough sailor types.

TRAVESTIS: Transvestites; drag queens [Variant name: *Drageurs*.]

Paris' queer venues ran the gamut from barebones, like *la Mère Gilbert*, a cheap and virtually undetectable working-class tavern, three blocks from the Saint-Michel metro, to the extravagant — notably *Chez Roland*, a super-luxurious night-club-cum-brothel, where a bottle of Clicquot Champagne cost exactly twice as much as the services of one of the Adonis-faced showboys.

In the early and mid-twenties, most of the same-sex bars and dance halls were located around Pigalle, usually within walking distance of the Moulin Rouge. In a typical night out, pairs or trios of gay men strolled from one honky-tonk to the next. Fynes Harte-Harrington, a British tourist, candidly recorded one of these evenings in an April 1923 diary entry:

We move to a venue called Chez Ma Cousine, at the top of Rue Lepic (behind the Moulin Rouge). Here we have a rather raucous time drinking and dancing. It is full of a wide range of different people. But nothing is what it appears and it is difficult to deduce which of the bewildering array of glamorous women are real women. I am staring at one in particular sat opposite us who looks vaguely familiar and the recognition annoys me.

"*What are you staring at?*" he says in a loud feminine voice in English.

"*You my dear. You are quite beautiful!*"

"*What do you expect, mon chéri. I am the star of this place!*" he says blowing me a kiss as he swivels around on the arms of a very dashing young man who winks at me with a big grin.

"*You have no idea who I am do you?*"

ABOVE LEFT: Jeanne Mammen, *La Mère Gilbert*, 1927

ABOVE RIGHT: Dugo, *This Dancer is Really Too Feminine* (Chez Roland), 1929

ABOVE: Léon Bonnotte, "At the *Chez Tonton*," 1930 (Two *Frappes*)

RIGHT: Brodsky, *Le Binocle in Full Swing*, 1939

OPPOSITE, CLOCKWISE FROM TOP LEFT: André Digimont, *Jésus la Caille*, 1929; A *"Travesti* at *La Triboulette*," 1939; Gaston Smitt, "Fredi's Amusement," 1920 (An *Amateur* with an *Entretenu*); "Don't worry! It's just a Christmas candle from Normandy," *Paris Sex-Appeal* (May 1934) (Two *Petits Messieurs*); Fabien Fabiano, "Apparently, he ignores the street signs," 1929 (A *Femme Entretenu*); "Playing in the Room," 1920 (A pornographic vision of *Petits Jésus*)

Suddenly the voice registers.

"Julian! Oh my, oh my. Fancy seeing you here…."

We are soon introduced by Julian (who is called Lucile) to many of 'her' friends. All had women's names and all were equally glamorous. Although I have to confess some had not perfected the illusion as well as Lucile, who was wearing an expensive white satin gown from Patou along with some stunning diamond accessories.

"These are real diamonds you know," says Lucile. *"My companion, Emile is heir to a fortune. Not that that is particularly an issue since I am too!!!"*

Lorenzo and I dance together and to my surprise he kisses me. No-one bats an eyelid. It is a difficult thing to understand, but I feel really good about it.

—After Dark: Fynes Harte-Harrington Website, 2009

Like the heterosexual *dancings*, many gay nightclubs fabricated distinct entertainment or environmental themes. *L'Isis* presented Tarabin-like cancan displays, although with appropriate drag flair. *Chez mon beau-frère* attempted to replicate the *Eldorado*, that celebrated Berlin transvestite institution in 1935. But it was lambasted as a pale imitation (the original German phantasmagoria had already gone out of business three years earlier when the Nazi menace first spread its homophobic venom). And queer tangos from pre-Franco Barcelona were energetically revived at *Le Binocle* following the collapse of the Spanish Republic.

Throughout the thirties, Fascist coups across Europe and their suppression of unconventional divertissements had altered the commercial face of Paris' vivacious party scene.

A TAXONOMY OF GAY MEN IN PARIS

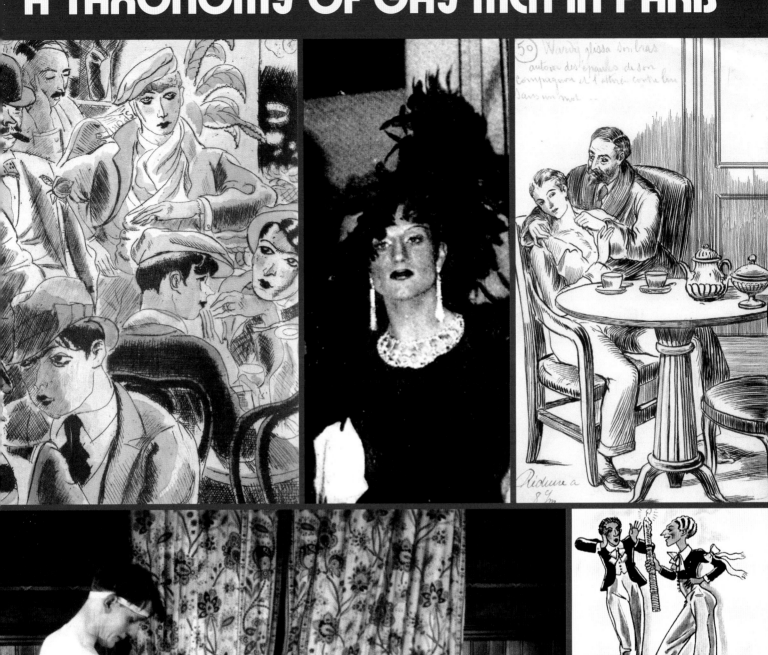

LIBERTY'S BAR

LEFT: Jean Cocteau, *Self-Portrait at Liberty's*, 1923

MIDDLE: Performer at Liberty's, 1925

RIGHT: Transvestite Chanteuse at Liberty's Bar, 1939

The most fearless and public of Paris' gay nightclubs, *Liberty's Bar*, was listed in the travel books as a *cabaret mondain*. Its queer habitués normally referred to it by the owner's name. Before 1919, the tiny Montmartre boîte was known as *Chez Palmyre* or the *Palmyrium*, after its tribadic landlord Madame Palmyre. Colette was a regular then and wrote engagingly about its freewheeling girl-on-girl milieu. In fact, her first physical relationship with a lesbian began here with a kiss on a bar stool.

After the war, the new title-holders, Bob Giguet, a blonde *drageur chanteuse*, and his/her dance partner Jean d'Albret, transformed the cramped bar into a charming little club restaurant, christened *Liberty's Bar*. (To the old-timers, it was just *Chez Bob et Jean*.) The new enterprise, like the neighboring jazz joints on Place Blanche, was brightly illuminated and brash, except Liberty's employed no American blacks, sabered Cossacks, or Argentines. Bobette and Jean had renovated the dim pickup saloon into a wacky transvestite ballroom and *lopette* showcase.

The Liberty's fan base was substantial and equally wacky: young queer writers (including Jean Cocteau), theatre folk, journalists, rakish French aristocrats, and even a few government ministers. Its dizzying shenanigans brought in wholesale clusters of tourists and curiosity-seekers. On weekends, at least one-third of the customers were straight couples.

Around ten o'clock, the *travesti* circus commenced. Bobette introduced each professional number, usually beginning with the flaming, broken-toothed, Spanish dancer Otéro. Between the acts, the showoff waiters slipped on chorus girl outfits and floppy hats before they pranced around the main floor. Their quick-draw transformations impeded the service but most spectators adored the ridiculous lampoon of the more serious-hearted burlesque performers.

Bobette and Jean bowed out of the Pigalle cabaret scene in 1940 but Liberty's transvestite antics continued through the German occupation — although under subdued circumstances — and revived again after the Allied liberation. The drag shows finally stopped when the bar changed hands in 1956.

LA PETITE CHAUMIÈRE

La Petite Chaumière was the closest Paris had to a no-holds-barred, Berlin-like transvestite club. A small rustic cottage (hence the name) with turkey-red cotton squares that covered its cross-hatched windows, it flourished two blocks from the Sacré-Cœur. The queer fortress was a labeled a "vestibule of unconcealed amusement." Like Liberty's, the Chaumière attracted both cross-dressing exhibitionists and het spectators yet here the crowds were of a more mixed multitude. Even its antechamber reeked of wafts of heavy perfumes permeated with men's sweat.

The sexual atmospherics at the Chaumière radiated otherworldly contrasts. There were gangs of identically attired fairies in slicked-back hair and smoking jackets. The vain *mignons* willfully ignored the *travestis*, in mismatched feminine wardrobes, who performed arabesques across the packed dance floor. (In 1925, a circle of chic *garçonnes* vaselined their shorn bobbed hair into a flat androgynous style. The novel coif was comically tagged the "Petite Chaumière.")

When a pianist banged out chords to a shimmy, Sissy-Boys in padded silk dresses and pearls or dainty kimonos sang in falsetto and shrieked in little-girl voices, "*Scotché, ma chère!*" They obscenely bumped bellies and sashayed about while pinching their crotches. All of this was directed at the smiling *visiteurs* and at Monsieur Tagada, the ever-content proprietor, and his sergeant-at-arms, the cigar-smoking Madame Maillot.

Roberts (gay hustlers), pickpockets, and some straight *danseurs de Madame* made their way through the crowds. The music was punctuated with an occasional sound of groping hands being slapped under the tables. Most striking and controversial were the Petite Chaumière's naughty midnight theatricals.

In May 1926, the *Sûreté* cut short one of the Chaumière ballets and arrested everyone in the cottage. Titled *The Sainted Mother Marie*, the show, an over-the-top gay parody, recreated a deplorable real-life

LEFT: A *Travesti* Performs, 1927

MIDDLE: *La Petite Chaumière* Ad, 1924

RIGHT: *Choosing a Dress*, 1931

BELOW: *The Flower-Lady*, 1931

scandal. The original event, which was covered extensively in the tabloid press, involved a sadistic Mother Superior from the infamous Notre Dame des Pleurs Order, a postulant nun-in-training, invective tongue-lashing, forced nudity, and a public flogging before a jeering assembly of matronly Sisters.

In the Chaumière version, a strapping Italian teen enacted the part of the Mme. Mesmin, the chief flagellant. Decked out in a white wimple and starched habit, he brandished a knotted rope and was trailed by a corps of twenty young men in similar getup (with their lips painted, cheeks rouged, and eyebrows plucked).

The crazed nuns stripped a comely actress, who played the part of the innocent Abbé des Noyers, tied her to a stake, and gloated over her naked vulnerability as they savagely whipped her. A few hours after the *Vaches* dragged the performers and spectators down to a Montmartre police station, the night-court judge dismissed the charges and faintly admonished the participants for their "indelicate" stage presentation.

The Chaumière, like most of the gay clubs in Paris, was under constant police surveillance. The *agents des mœurs* tolerated "discreet" amounts of prostitution at these venues and monitored their sometimes wayward decorum but the blasphemous Chaumière productions triggered a more ham-fisted verdict. The *Préfet de Police*, responding to a series of formal complaints beginning in 1925, fined the cottage's owners and temporarily sealed its doors. In 1931, the Petite Chaumière was officially proscribed, shuttered, and Tagada's license revoked.

ABOVE: Bécan, *Evening at the Petite Chaumière*, 1929

CHEZ TONTON

Gaston Baheux (1897–1966) launched *Chez Tonton*, the last of the legendary homosexual boutique bars, in 1930. A former transvestite performer at the Petite Chaumière and Liberty's and master showman in his own right, Monsieur Tonton formally inaugurated his tony establishment with a "parade of flowers," a line of naked boys wearing ridiculous wigs. From the start, Uncle Tonton conjured up a gendered *monde* turned upside down.

Chez Tonton ladled out a *bouillabaisse* of fun attractions, including *drageur* musical sketches by Serge Davri Charpini (the "male soprano") and O'dett. The high-voltage duo expertly mimicked Paris' superstars, such as Colette, Fréhel, and Mistinguett (Chez Tonton's patron saint) and all their eccentric mannerisms. The gracious *chassonniers,* who often joined the after-midnight crowds, hailed their male imitators.

On the sidelines, Tonton and his sidekick Nono sauntered around the club disguised as sanctimonious straight dandies. They pompously taunted the performers about their physical and vocal imperfections.

One of the club *travestis*, "Madame Butterfly," remained in character through the evenings. She sat primly on the spectators' laps, reciting from Racine's *Phèdre* or some other Neoclassical tragedy. The operatic *chanteuse* bemoaned the death of imperial France in 1789, blaming the present-day Communist Party for the sorry state of events and her debased artistic status.

Months before the German invasion in 1940, Monsieur Tonton took over the Liberty and succeeded in keeping both emporiums of deviance operating at full throttle during the four Black Years. Miss, from the get-go and through the Occupation, was a backstage presence at Tonton's cabarets and supported his madcap ventures. After the Libération, Nono recorded a paean to the showstopping idol, "A Woman is Always a Woman." It quickly became the informal anthem of Paris' resuscitated underworld of hustlers and black-market entrepreneurs.

ABOVE LEFT: Doorman at *Chez Tonton*, 1931

ABOVE MIDDLE: Charpini and O'dett at the *Chez Tonton*, 1930

ABOVE RIGHT: *Tonton and Friends Under a Canvas by Kiki de Montparnasse*, 1930

BELOW: Bar and Lounge at *Chez Tonton*, 1931

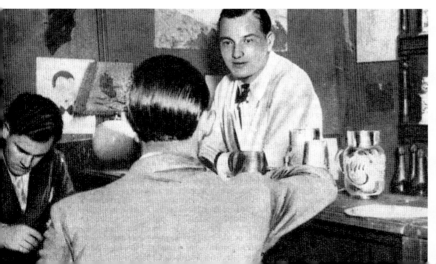

MAGIC CITY NIGHTS

LEFT: Brassaï, *One Suit For Two*, 1931

RIGHT: Brassaï, *Bal du Magic City*, 1933

Publicists for *Magic City* promoted its ballroom as the most spacious in Paris proper, its lighting system as a world marvel, and its house orchestra as nothing less than incomparable. Located in the outlying 7th *Arrondissement*, two blocks from the Seine, Magic City's warehouse-sized main floor did impress. Versailles-like windows framed the dance hall and enormous nineteenth-century chandeliers were bolted to its sky-high ceilings. Yet the dance palace's interwar repute had little to do with its architectural or artistic wonders. Magic City was largely in the news and on the lips of closeted homosexuals due to its mid-Lenten transvestite carnival.

From 1922 until 1934, the annual *drageur* ball drew thousands of exuberant celebrants into Magic City's one-night Mardi Gras vortex. Many gay men, who customarily obscured their sexual inclinations from workmates and neighbors,

spent veritable fortunes on extravagant theatrical gear. Feathered hats, dangling silver earrings, and sequined *froufrous* were commonplace uniforms. Others dressed like gangster-like *pédés*, sailors, or moseyed about as partially disrobed versions of themselves.

ABOVE: Brodsky, a team of *Pipes* on parade and one *Petit Garçon*, 1939

Although Magic City's same-sex fêtes totaled only thirteen over the years, Brassaï immortalized them when he published a pictorial series of the unconstrained revelers — together with similar impromptu images from the *Bal de la Salle Wagram* — in 1933. Predictably, the *Bureau des Mœurs,* to prevent further public embarrassment, banned the Rabelaisian evenings altogether. During the mid-thirties and long after, Brassaï's strikingly empathetic visuals acquired considerable panache among the artistic set and have remained indelible imprints of queer Paris in holiday (or truly liberated) mode.

UNDER WRAPS AND ON THE STREET

Beyond the *pissoirs* (or *vespasiennes*), gay men seeking anonymous sexual contacts could obtain them on the sly in Turkish bathhouses and massage parlors. There were fifteen of these marbled temples scattered around the city. A few of them, like the *Bains d'Angoulême*, near the Place de la Bastille, could accommodate more than one hundred patrons by the hour.

After dipping into private tubs of scalding or chilled water, the solitary bathers silently entered a darkened chamber that was filled with pumped-in steam. Sitting on tiled slabs of circular steps, the naked strangers pressed against each other in the thickly fogged room until they formed a tangled human pyramid. During their fifteen-minute orgasmic embrace, most of them achieved a satisfactory communal sexual union. Later the nude lovers draped their bodies in Roman-style togas and

GLOSSARY OF LESBIAN TYPES

AMAZONES: Masculine women.

DAMES SEULES ("Women Alone"): Fashionable gay ladies.

GARÇONNES: Bob-haired tomboys or women who dressed and behaved like men. [A term that changed meaning after 1928.]

GOUINES: Bull dykes with monocles in mannish outfits.

GOULUES ("Swallowers"): Women who have oral sex with other women.

GOUSSES ("Pods"): Fat lesbians; butches.

MONOS (Abbreviation for "Monosexuals"): Slim, Eton-cropped young same-sexers.

TRIBADES: Generic term for lesbians.

ABOVE: Lucien Jaquelux, *A New Race, the "Monosexuals,"* 1923

RIGHT: Maurice Barte, *The Flirt,* 1930

HOMOSEXUAL TYPES IN THE SEX TRADE

DOMESTICS: Young procurers of *Petits jésus.* [Variant name: *Femmes de chambre.*]

ENTRETENUS: Rent boys employed by rich queers.

FILLES GALANTES: Teenagers controlled by a *Souteneur.*

GARÇONS DE PLAISIR: Homosexual prostitutes. [Variant name: *Minets.*]

MAUVAIS GARÇONS ("Bad Boys"): Aggressive hustlers; corner-boys. [Variant name: *Voyous.*]

PERSILLEUSES: Gay hookers who approached women in order to borrow their rooms.

PETITS GARÇONS: Transvestite male streetwalkers.

PIERREUSES: Husky outdoor sirens.

PIPES ("Penises"): Bottom-drawer hustlers, usually seen in packs.

RIVETTES: Amateur pickups.

dined on wooden picnic tables. While they caroused and partied during the feast, a pianist and folksinger belted out raunchy versions of familiar street ballads.

Male prostitution was largely confined to the interiors and immediate surroundings of gay clubs and deep inside the *bois*. Patrolmen, even in Montmartre, took a dim view of the *garçons de plaisir* when they congregated anywhere near the winding pathways where tourists may have drunkenly wandered. No matter. By the end of the thirties, the favorite gathering spots of the open-air *pipes* and *bobs,* usually near train stations and gated parks, had been unearthed by yellow journalists. The reporters blamed it on the Republic's porous borders and poorly regulated immigration policies. The indigenous *rivettes* knew their proper place in the city's genteel thoroughfares.

LESBIANS IN PLAIN SIGHT

Lesbians always had a visible presence in Paris. In the heart of the city, in its 1st *Arrondissement*, there were three restricted tea rooms, *Thé Colombin, Le Wagram,* and *Thé Récamier,* where ladies in designer cloches and exquisite frocks sipped *aperitifs,* shared gossip, and tastefully flirted. At the Colombin, they smoked from half-meter-long pipes that hung from the salon's newspaper racks.

The publication of Margueritte's *La Garçonne* in 1922 spotlighted the sexual vitality of *lesbiennes* in their Montmartre and high-society habitats. In a blink, *tribades* were accorded France's greatest stamp of approval: they were erotically charged with newfangled and alluring possibilities. Whatever *dames seules* did in bed was the focus of intense heterosexual concern.

Female third-sexers themselves awoke to their overnight status as sexual innovators and began to circulate in the city's nightlife. Most lesbian social clubs and parlors duplicated already booming ventures — just with a different clientele. Yet that too changed.

ABOVE LEFT: Lesbian dancers in the *Rive Gauche,* 1931

ABOVE RIGHT: Georges Pavis, *In the Foyer of the Empire Music-Hall,* 1933

LESBIAN CLUBS

LE FÉTICHE

Just a sprinkling of lesbian clubs devised inventive lay-outs or dedicated ambiances that signaled their tribadic mission. The earliest to appear in Montmartre was Monique Carton's *Le Fétiche*. Pink and black Cubist designs adorned the restaurant and tiny bar. Artificial roses and symbolic murals of a cat, crow, and unicorn by Sacha Zaliouk were painted or pinned to the walls. The unicorn (which could only be caught by a virgin, according to French folklore) had two horns in Zaliouk's rendering, a playful depiction of lesbian virtue.

Outside, the sensuous blonde doorwoman, Petit Louis, and her charming assistant inspected all the incoming merchandise. A peppery *garçonne*, Louis did not conceal her distaste for the whole unseemly panorama.

Monique introduced cabaret acts on weekends and diners threw streamers at the dancing couples when their embraces got too steamy to ignore. It was said that *Le Fétiche's* foyer contained more beautiful

women per square meter than any place in Paris, although Anaïs Nin found the *dames seules* overly masculine and unappealing. Gorgeous or not, a cadre of *Le Fétiche* regulars had wed stay-at-home *mignons*, who cared for their children at night.

LA PERLE

Across the street in Pigalle, an upscale lesbian restaurant-club catered to a decidedly more voracious and sex-hungry crowd. This was the elitist hangout *La Perle*. Noisy and fast-paced, it was an unintentional caricature of the predatory straight cabarets along Boulevard de Clichy.

Super-male *gouines* in high collars and tuxes gyrated breast-to-breast with their frilly dates. As a recognized pickup joint for wealthy *femmes*, la Perle enticed wannabe dykes in search of one-night stands as well as swinging couples on the make. Jealous displays and emotional outbursts frequently upended the jaunty bandleader's proclamations in the late hours.

LE MONOCLE

Like Martoune, the operator of the Sphinx brothel, Lulu de Montparnasse envisioned an ultra-moderne concession of decadence in the artistic 14th *Arrondissement*, far from touristy Montmartre. *Le Monocle,* her pioneering lesbian outpost,

TOP LEFT: Brassaï, *Lulu's Table at Le Monocle*, 1932

TOP RIGHT: Brassaï, *Fat Claude with Her Girlfriend*, 1932

BOTTOM LEFT: Brassaï, *Lesbian Couples at Le Monocle*, 1932

BOTTOM RIGHT: *Le Monocle* Scene

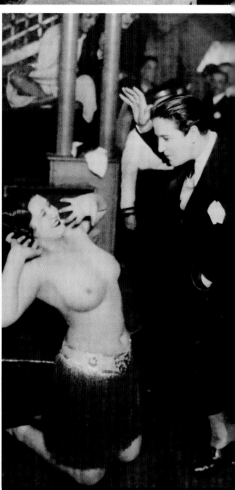

kicked off in 1931. Its name referred to the nineteenth-century male accoutrement that *gouines* had proudly sported as their facial calling card.

Acclaimed as "Paris' prominent masculine figure," Lulu wanted her cabaret to serve as the *au courant* "temple of Sapphic love." She hired attractive, doe-eyed hostesses and encouraged smutty *tête-à-têtes*. Lulu herself hit on any wistful beauty that temporally isolated herself by the bar or in Le Monocle's disreputable ladies' room. On a miniature side stage, an all-girl orchestra played hit-parade medleys and backup for the club's improvised sketch comedy.

Brassaï, as he had with the Magic City *bals*, captured the funhouse spontaneity of the place. Among his intimate portraits were several of a mannish creature whom he captioned "Fat Claude." In fact, the hyper-*amazone* was none other than Violette Morris, France's multifaceted celebrity athlete and, later during the Occupation, single most reviled female collaborator employed by the Gestapo.

SUZY SOLIDOR AND *LA VIE PARISIENNE*

In the lesbian *demi-monde*, only one performer managed to straddle the confines of that cozy inbred network and *le Tout-Paris*. This was the "French Dietrich," Suzy Solidor (1900–1986). Acknowledged as the sweet Gallic face (and baritone voice) of contemporary *tribadisme*, "the tigress with flaxen hair" candidly broadcast her *invert* lifestyle and bisexual conquests. Suzy's barroom banter, heartfelt crooning, and unique repertoire were heralded for their outrageously intimate and dramatic qualities.

The illegitimate daughter of a *restaurateur* who claimed to be a descendent of a heroic seventeenth-century buccaneer, Suzy left her native Bretagne to become a model in Paris. At the end of World War I, she drove an ambulance wagon and, in the twenties, made the rounds of nightclubs and revue houses as a minor

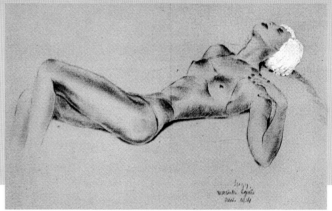

chanteuse and walk-on *figurante*. Suzy's command of provincial seafaring songs and unusual *garçonne* appearance brought her to the attention of budding composers and amateur music-hall financiers.

In December 1932, Suzy opened *La Vie Parisienne*, a small but vibrant cabaret two blocks west of the Bibliothéque Nationale. Swarms of androgynous couples, elegant socialites, culture mavens, and testy tomboys formed the club's core aficionados. Pundits immediately pronounced la Vie "a schoolroom out of *Mädchen in Uniform*," the German film that disclosed the sexual proclivities of lesbian academics and their rebellious pupils.

Accompanied by Henri Brey on the piano, Suzy sang bubbly ditties, genderless tearjerkers about abusive relationships, sea shanties, javas, and full-throated harbor-girl laments. An out *tapette*, Brey teased the *mono* heartthrob with proposals of marriage and engaged, *sotto voce*, in a barrage of ironic repartee between sets. The mood quickly shifted from sassy improvisation to romantic longing to piquant revelation.

In 1938, a record studio released Suzy's signature vocal, "L'Escale" ("The Port")

in a cleaned-up version and the altered ballad became an instant hit on French radio. When Suzy performed the lyrically scrubbed standard at la Vie, her ardent fans responded to the censored text ("The sky is blue, the sea is green, open your window a bit") by chanting the original naughty refrain: "The sky is blue, the sea is green, open your sailorboy fly a bit."

Suzy Solidor managed to eke out success in the public sphere — she was cast in three musical films — while her nightclub thrived as an authentic bastion of promiscuous female sexuality.

Graphic artists from a dozen countries, in countless styles, attempted to depict Suzy's singular persona on canvas. La Vie's walls were overlaid with forty portraits of the ephebic siren. (During the thirties and forties, more than two hundred were presented to her.) Up-and-coming painters jostled to place their framed compositions of Mlle. Solidor in the cabaret gallery that stretched from the "washroom to the cash register." A Greek-like statue of the living goddess rested on a pedestal by the stage backdrop. And the club's bartender kept a stack of pictorial booklets of the Suzy-scape on his zinc counter.

SOUPERS·DINERS·DÉJEUNERS

A TOUTE HEURE

chez

Graff

Place Blanche
(contre le Moulin Rouge)

le Restaurant de Montmartre
renommé pour ses spécialités
et sa clientèle d'artistes

OUVERT TOUTE LA NUIT

André Luguet et Alice Field soupent chez GRAFF

Chez Suzy was a favorite hangout of Cocteau and Jean Gabin, who once dragged Marlene Dietrich there after a theatre performance. Mainstream lesbian writers and intellectuals frowned upon the bombshell's snicker-inducing megalomania and avoided la Vie Parisienne *en masse*. Some claimed that the side-by-side renderings of the blonde enchantress practically made them seasick.

MIXED CABARETS AND BARS

Despite its broad appeal, la Vie Parisienne was clearly designated as a lesbian nightclub. Others, like *Chez Graff* and *Le Bœuf sur le toit*, fell into more circumspective categories. A late-night retreat for *montmartroises* and their *mecs,* the Graff equally attracted gay couples and cross-dressed revelers, who drunkenly waddled from table to table. This was also the prime morning destination for Magic City's *travestis*.

The Alsatian owner, Louis Moysès, named Le Bœuf after Cocteau and Darius Milhaud's 1920 satirical ballet, *Ox on the Roof*. Reportedly this was the first place where American jazz was heard. Maddening to hotshot travelers, this tony *brasserie* was forced to relocate four times: the first transfer because neighbors complained about Cocteau's percussive pounding on the orchestra's drums at 2 a.m. After each move, it became increasing upscale and increasingly fey. In the end, it was the main watering hole for gay intellectuals, the *haute pédale*.

The two chief entertainers from Chez Tonton, Charpini and O'dett, opened their own separate *boîtes* toward the end of the thirties. Although their transvestite personas and musical parodies hadn't much changed in practice since Tonton engaged them, their audiences were now mostly

OPPOSITE TOP: A parody of *Carmen* at *Chez O'dett*, 1936

OPPOSITE MIDDLE: Charpini and Brancato at *Chez Charpini*, 1939

OPPOSITE BOTTOM: *Chez Graff* business card, 1932

LEFT: Gerda Wegener, *Chez Graff*, 1926

die-hard heterosexuals. Queer humor had bound from its humble environs to become Paris' newest trend.

Jean Genet, then a thirty-year-old gay hustler and fledgling novelist, remembered O'dett, in a "strange revue" at the ABC Music-Hall, giving his spot-on impression of a wildly gesticulating Hitler. This was in January 1940, in the midst of France's "phony war." Six months later, the Führer himself would be flown to a conquered Paris. He was filmed staring at the Eiffel Tower, standing stiffly with his arms braced against his resplendent Nazi tunic. ❖

EROTO-MANIA

It [the Bal des Quat'z' Arts] is a riot, a revival of paganism, known elsewhere only in Italy. It is also, in its way, a hymn to beauty, a living explosion of the senses and the emotions.

— E. Berry Wall, *Neither Pest Nor Puritan*, 1940 —

Sacred coitus opens the portal to heaven. But to pass through the gate, women must offer themselves completely without ego. That is the great secret of Love Magic [...] Woman can be either Mother or Priestess. The Mother conceives physically; the Priestess gives birth to the Illumination of Sex.

— Henri Meslin, *Theory and Practice of Sex Magic*, 1938 —

CHAPTER

7

TO STRANGERS, PARIS APPEARED TO BE a chimera of furtive sexual desires. And the city fathers, like proud engineers, seemed to have little incentive to regulate them. Adulterers, creators and consumers of pornography, fetishists, aficionados of underage prostitutes, philandering businessmen, and homosexuals on the prowl were all tolerated entities in the city's boundless and eroticized social fabric. The French even had a term for private arrangements devised by couples seeking new or multiple partners: *partouzes*. For the denizens of the love capital, it was simply a matter of place, proper decorum, and class status.

OPPOSITE: *Bal Bullier* in the Latin Quarter, 1934

Le premier hebdomadaire des faits-divers

6ᵉ Année - Nᵒ 268   1 FR. 50 - TOUS LES JEUDIS - 16 PAGES   14 Décembre 1933

DÉTECTIVE

Les «dédrogués»

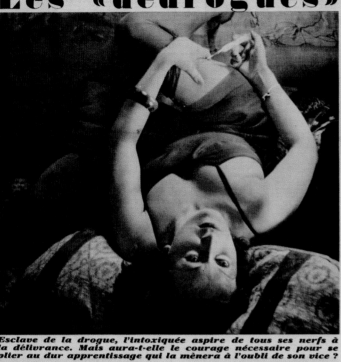

Esclave de la drogue, l'intoxiquée aspire de tous ses nerfs à la délivrance. Mais aura-t-elle le courage nécessaire pour se plier au dur apprentissage qui la mènera à l'oubli de son vice ?
(Lire, page 14, le sensationnel reportage de notre collaborateur René B. Castelot.)

AU SOMMAIRE | Entr'acte, par Marcel Montarron. – Si les forçats, un jour..., par Paul Bringuier – Lynchage-partie, par Roy Pinker. – Femmes DE CE NUMÉRO | jugées, par Maggie Guiral et Jean Morières. – Monnaie de singe, par Emmanuel Car. – Pègre des mers, par Etienne Hervier.

But Paris, in league with other Western cities, had defined carnal boundaries. Any exploitive behaviors linked to incest, psychological manipulation, imprisonment, drugs, or physical violence were severely sanctioned. Stories about such moral transgressions were the bread and butter of the pulp press. In weekly homilies, they agonized over the wretched victims and recounted the legal proceedings against the heinous defilers of the Napoleonic criminal code.

French authorities were equally appalled by some accepted and common sex practices in other lands. To their dismay, despite assistance from the *police de Sûreté*, they were unable to tamp down the salacious allure of these uncouth foreign customs or suppress their local adherents.

Organized nudism, for instance, escalated into a communal fad in Germany in the 1920s, drawing the participation of millions of health fanatics and ordinary middle-class families. Its precepts increasingly influenced German notions of well-being and the platforms of its revolutionary political parties. In Paris, public nudity, although a comic enterprise to most, was denounced and savagely prosecuted in its courts.

Erotomania, or sexual obsession, emerged in a maze of inimitable French forms. Lust and fashion-conscious pageantry fused with antiquated Gallic festivals, anti-Christian rites, *Mittel-European* clubs of naked life reformers, neo-pagan religions, and modern love cults.

Paris — denuded or heretical — was still Paris.

NAKED BALLS

Student and artists' balls in the Latin Quarter during *la Belle Époque* were thought by *agents des mœurs* to be spur-of-the-moment bashes. For the most part, they broke out during the week preceding the Baccalauréat exams and were said to be terpsichorean discharges from intensive study.

Some historians, however, insisted that the delirious revelries were not at all spontaneous. They were scholarly attempts to resuscitate the mid-Lenten celebrations that once inflamed medieval Paris. And like the eleventh-century Feast of Fools and Boy Bishop Day — holidays that so vexed the ecclesiastic prefects — these

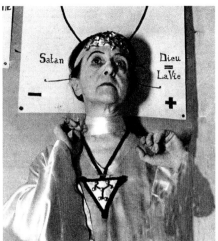

galas quickly expanded in scope and indecent tomfoolery. (Imitating the coarse Roman Saturnalias that they were supposed to replace, the spring free-for-alls turned the temples of the worship into bawdy funhouses of riotous drinking, erotic bullying, and obscene merrymaking: human feces and urine were often poured into holy vessels as substitutes for communion wafers and wine.)

The *Bal des Quat'z' Arts* (*4 Z'Arts*) was, by far, the best-known of the student procession-and-masked-ball extravaganzas. Begun in the 1890s by pupils from the École des Beaux Arts, the organizers of the annual event awarded prizes (of Champagne) for the most artistic or daring costume handiwork. After the banquet and midnight dance, the celebrants rushed into the streets, leaping on parked

OPPOSITE MIDDLE: Artists' Ball in Montparnasse, 1929

OPPOSITE BOTTOM: Ferdinand Kòra, *Quat'z' Arts Ball*, 1929

ABOVE LEFT: Mécano, *Kiki at an Artists' Ball*, 1929

ABOVE CENTER: Stéphane Pisella, *Maria de Naglowska, High Priestess of a Luciferian Sex Cult*, 1935

ABOVE RIGHT: Canteloup-Sabrou, *Bal des Quat'z' Arts* Invitation: "The Glorious Reign of Nebuchadnezzar," 1933

LEFT: R.P., *Bal des Quat'z' Arts* Invitation: "The Victorious Homecoming in Athens after the Battle of Salamis," 1931

vehicles and statue pedestals. The student flashers exposed their breasts and *derrières* to shocked passers-by. The 4 Z'Arts always concluded with a flotilla of indoor Mardi Gras-like floats, followed by a "drunken orgy of naked bodies" and mad sprints into the Seine by those still able to stand.

Although the ball and after-hours carnival was a private affair and restricted to apprentice architects, painters, sculptors, and engravers enrolled at the École, police and conservative politicians took a dim view of the rowdy free-for-all. Twice they attempted to halt the street parade, fining and imprisoning its leaders and a few of the nude models. Riots and tragedy ensued. A patrolman picked up an errant cobblestone and hurtled it back into the mob. The granite block struck a student in the head, killing him instantly. Thirty thousand troops had to be summoned to restore order.

In the end, the yearly mayhem of the 4 Z'Arts fêtes endured, unimpeded by irate lawmen or uptight chamber deputies. It soon became one of Paris' largest and most anticipated attractions.

Each 4 Z'Arts had a roguish historical motif that was supposed to be reflected in the overall design, costume choices, and musical accompaniments. After receiving that season's woodcut invitation, printed in eye-catching hues, a Beaux Arts attendant would know whether to gear up as a Phoenician sailor, Hun horseman, sacrificial virgin to an Inca god, cowboy, Cambodian empress, or Athenian warrior. This very singular art event inspired a dozen copycat all-nighters in France and abroad. And like so much of louche Paris, it lasted until 1939 and then resurfaced in a diminished format in 1946.

THE UNFETTERED BODY

Twenty miles northwest of Paris, on the island of Médan, a naturalist village, *Physiopolis*, was painstakingly banged together in 1925.

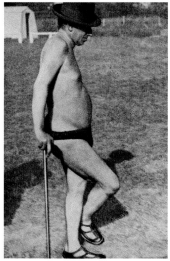

TOP: Robert Charroux, *Isle of Beauty*, 1934

BOTTOM ROW: Charles Rapho, *Société Naturiste*, 1932

Established by the physicians André and Gaston Durville, the isle was the center-piece of their physical culture association, *Société Naturiste*. Pastoral and serene, Physiopolis could only be reached by ferry and was the one authorized clothes-free bathing area in the vicinity of Paris.

Médan's beaches and bungalows were packed on weekends. Over three thousand sun-worshipping Parisians made the journey during warm-weather Sundays. But in the opinion of France's traditional nudists, this manufactured speck of Eden was "a vulgar spectacle," just a pathetic Coney Island on the Seine.

In compliance with municipal decrees for civic propriety, full nudity was not permitted at Physiopolis. Men wore dark tunics or specially designed *loiners* — impractical, triangular-shaped loincloths that barely covered their genitalia. Women veiled their breasts and pubic regions with black silk brassières and chemises called "modesty belts." These peculiar garments suggestively accentuated the portions of the body that were supposed to be hidden.

Under the naked sky, chartered members of the Société Naturiste could partake in Swedish gymnastics, track-and-field-like sports, same-sex wrestling, dips in the icy Seine, picnicking, and interpretative dance. Yet there was a manifest puritanical aspect to the Physiopolis regimen. Alcohol was forbidden as well as meat. And, at night, children, men, and women were shunted into segregated encampment sites.

Since the Durvilles only indirectly endorsed *le culte de la nudité*, their biweekly journals, *La Vie Sage* and *Naturisme,* were freely displayed throughout Paris. The magazine covers never flaunted any naked-as-jaybirds nature-lovers, only photographs of frolicking Adams and Eves in tasteful black bikinis.

TOP: Charles Rapho, *Ligue Vivre Intégralement*, 1934

ABOVE: *Société Naturiste* Necklace, 1936

RIGHT: Bertram, *Sparta Club*, 1934

Despite the colony's virtuous protocol and many erotic restrictions, an infant girl was born on the island in 1933, the first in two hundred years. Her parents named her "Physiopolis."

The *Ligue Vivre Intégralement* proffered a more aggressive approach to nudism. Marcel Kienné de Mongeot, a Nordic-looking aviator who claimed Jeanne d'Arc as an ancestor, and Yvan de Laval founded the league in 1920. Both believed that outdoor nudity in rural surroundings was a natural health aid and drug-free therapy for tuberculosis. They proselytized naked air and sunbathing as essential restoratives borrowed from classical Greek medicine.

Like the Société Naturiste, which de Mongeot derided as an ersatz nudist organization, the *Ligue Vivre Intégralement* had its own publishing arm, magazine, and headquarters located within Paris. Most of its social gatherings, however, took place at a private county estate, ninety minutes from the city. Its official organ, *Vivre Intégralement*, which featured philosophical treatises on hardy primitive life-styles, the international nudist movement, and pictures of glorious naked bodies, was under a partial ban. The monthly could be sold at newspaper stands and bookstores but not publicly exhibited on the shutters of Paris' kiosks.

If anything, police scrutiny and media skepticism — a torrent of cartoons in the newsweeklies spoofed the asexual rectitude of nudists and their leaders — actually increased interest in the Ligue's subterranean activities.

To join de Mongeot and de Laval's federation of "integral nudism," one had to be vouched for by a current associate. Between 1926 and 1930, over one hundred Masonic-like naturalist groups had sprung up across the French-speaking world. Altogether some sixty thousand card-carrying members shelled out five hundred *francs* each to parade around in their birthday suits and listen to de Mongeot's life-reform lectures.

The newly prosperous *Ligue Vivre Intégralement* established a sprawling colony, *Sparta-Club*, at a medieval *château* outside Garambouville. The sixteenth-century

Normandy castle was forty miles from the English Channel and two hours from Paris by rapid train and taxi. It contained dormitories, swimming pools, a mammoth park, and cavernous feudal hall as well as ultraviolet saunas and a walled "nudarium" for supervised heliotherapy treatments.

Unlike Physiopolis, Sparta-Club had few rules or constraints. Classes in Expressive Gymnastics were offered but not mandated. Dinners normally included wine, cheese, and meat entrees. (Sparta's novel breakfast elixir, something called yogurt, was served with fresh fruit.) Even tobacco smoking and erections were permitted, sometimes cropping up in tandem.

In 1944, before the D-Day invasion, splinter groups of extremist Freemasons and Theosophists challenged de Mongeot's *laissez-faire* and nonpolitical direction. They created their own clandestine nudist societies, *Club du Soleil* and the *Centre Héliomarin*.

LEFT: Jehan Sylvius, *Black Masses*, 1926

RIGHT: Black Mass at Chez Mme. Albert, 1928

THE BLACK MASS

Satan worship, the scourge of seventeenth-century France, took many ominous and secretive forms, none more troubling to the Church's hierarchy than the Black Mass. It was a reverse consecration of the Eucharist, conducted by dissident Catholic priests. Those ordained seminarians who chose to serve the Devil and "live in mortal sin" had not completely forsaken their priestly vows; they had merely changed deities. They led underground communities in the adoration of the "light-granting" Lucifer (renamed Satan after his descent into Hell).

The rites of the Black Mass were an ineffable blend of heathen folk ceremonies, extant Gnostic liturgy, traditional Catholic communion sacraments, Witches' Sabbaths, and ritualized sexual perversion. What seemed like a cultish mash-up of unholy and blasphemous practices quickly evolved into a formal service that commenced with prayers for the Devil's consent and blessings from his underworld minions. Clerics then goaded the Black Mass congregants into a rapturous state that terminated with an hour of general debauchery and group copulation.

Archbishops, parish priests, and special inquisitors appointed by the Holy See struggled to thoroughly quell the mass heresy. Most of the purveyors of witchcraft

and black magic were publicly tried and summarily executed. The last French priest convicted of sorcery and holding Black Masses was burnt at the stake in 1745.

Huysman revived Paris' fascination with Satanism and the Black Mass at the end of the nineteenth century but it was largely a literary undertaking. In 1903, the illustrated monthly *L'Assiette au Beurre* devoted an entire issue to the phenomenon. Of course, the Prince of Darkness cults were subjected to a comic treatment. The disciples of Satan were rebuked as "strange, sad imbeciles."

During the interwar period, however, Black Masses were accorded more substantial and serious coverage. They popped up in Montparnasse and Pigalle with some regularity. Usually, the demonic observances were mounted in outlying *maisons de rendez-vous* and took on theatrical trappings.

One such ceremony was filmed at *Chez Mme. Albert* in 1928 and later sold as a porno one-reeler. Mlle. Isabelle officiated over the conspiratorial proceedings, where she was said to have radiated a "weird incandescent glow." Her acolytes, besides the hooded priest, included professors, young devotees, and *filles de joie* with a religious/anti-religious bent. Several massive cathedrals towered over the brothel. The chiming of their bells was incorporated into the Satanic induction. (How well the sacrilegious featurette sold was anyone's guess.)

LEFT: René Thimmy, *Magic in Paris*, 1934

CENTER: *Votre Destin* (April 11, 1935)

RIGHT: *Madame X Receives a Supplicant*, 1935

BELOW: Brodsky, *In a Parlor of Satanic Love*, 1936

SEX MAGIC AND LOVE CULTS

Like many American and European cities, Paris had its share of magic circles, occult associations, and love cults. All of them eschewed rigid bourgeois notions of marital fidelity. Charismatic gurus and their subordinates vigilantly controlled the lives and intimate activities of their members and initiates. Some of them proselytized a belief system based on religious chastity; others piloted their laity into the higher realms of erotic consciousness or imposed a new sexualized pecking order on their disciples.

The most notorious, if little documented, sex cult was the *Cénacle d'Astaré*, located a few blocks east of the Arc de Triomphe. René Thimmy briefly mentioned the operation in his authoritative *La Magie à Paris* but a full description only came to light in the pages of *Stag* (January 1960). The American true crime monthly alleged unpublished files in the *Sûreté* as its source.

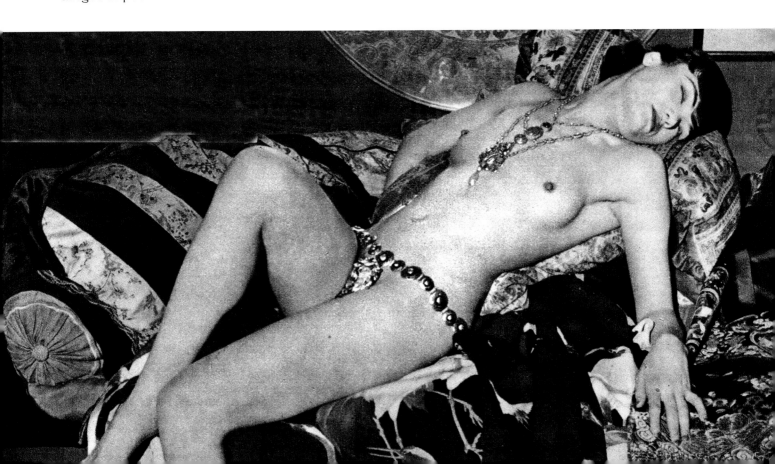

RIGHT: Emmet Kay, *Cénacle d'Astaré*, 1960

In the early 1920s, a gruff doorman stood guard inside the temple's foyer. Madame Crielle offered cups of drugged wine mixed with aphrodisiac herbs in the antechamber to male and female libertines from wealthy backgrounds, who comprised the bulk of her fellowship.

A large dark room with soft rugs and smoking braziers filled with hashish and ether was secreted in the center of the mansion. This was where the Cénacle inductees were directed.

A cone of red light illuminated an eight-foot marble statue of Astarté. The initiates were instructed to bow and chant before the black-robed priestess. The real action kicked off at the stroke of midnight. Couples were handed whips to aid them in rehearsed scenarios of flagellation and magical intercourse. According to Crielle, these experiments were devotional rites that she replicated from the Bronze Age fertility cult of Astarté, the Divine-Female.

The sixty-eight-year-old Madame Crielle was arrested in 1926 for the ritual murders of five young men. After hanging them upside down in front of the marble Astarté idol, she slit their wrists and drank the blood that flowed into iron vases. Crielle maintained that the men's blood acted as a rejuvenating elixir. She died at the Salpétrière hospital in February 1927, the consequence of "senile decay."

Rumors of psychosexual manipulation and other sinister forms of exploitation dogged many of the New Age communities that cropped up across Central and Western Europe before the Wall Street Crash. G.I. Gurdjieff's *Institute for the Harmonious Development of Man* was typical in this regard. The Russian-in-exile's outsize personality and esoteric teachings drew scores of titled aristocrats, Anglo-Saxon socialites, eminent artists and writers, philosophers and mathematicians to his Parisian classrooms and gorgeous villa near Fontainebleau, thirty-five miles south of the city.

ABOVE: Panini, *Gurdjieff's Society* "Chain Gang," 1926

Awoken at five in the morning and separated by gender, Gurdjieff's pupils were ordered to perform some vigorous task that eluded their everyday routine. For the social butterflies, this was generally backbreaking labor at the estate's quarry. A teetotalling pastor was forced to drink two magnums of Champagne in one sitting. The master commanded each participant to carry out some personally unfamiliar or distasteful action. (For this august privilege, they had to ante up two thousand *francs* per week.)

Afterwards the Institute disciples were tutored in exercises in "self-remembering" and Sacred Movements. Gurdjieff explained to journalists that this was "the Work." And accounts of the late-night Oriental-themed dances and sensual frolics did little to tarnish the cult's international reputation.

MARIA DE NAGLOWSKA AND THE CONFRÉRIE DE LA FLÈCHE D'OR

Between 1930 and 1936, another Russian mystic, Maria de Naglowska (1883–1936), cast a disquieting spell on Paris. Known as the "Sophia of Montparnasse," Naglowska preached an intriguing religio-erotic creed, "the Third Term of the Trinity." Her antinomian doctrine trisected the Godhead into divine archetypes that were linked to the evolution of faith in human history: first the religion of the Father (Judaism), the divisive male principle, where love seeks flesh; then the Son (Christianity), the neutral and passive principle, which rejects flesh completely; and finally the Mother (Naglowska's TTT), where love, raising from flesh, allows

mankind to achieve sublime purity. In the TTT phrase, the eternal war between God and Satan, at last, is reconciled and Jesus appropriately sanctified.

Naglowska could be found hawking her pamphlets and irregular newspaper, *La Flèche, Organe d'action magique,* in front of Montparnasse cafés. She implored curious spectators to witness the weekly services at her Brotherhood of the Golden Arrow. Police informants, competing occultists, and disbelieving journalists were all cheerfully welcomed.

Besides promoting Golden Arrow lectures and publications, Naglowska guided her congregation in the worship of the Demonic Woman. These venerations of *la Sagesse* were billed as a mysterious healing force and transformative means to self-deification. Her spiritual explorations liberally borrowed from the Black Mass and Cénacle group but they also contained other spiritual components. The Brotherhood, in her words, aspired to "crush the Snakehead of Masculine Satanism and insert the Solar Phallus into the mouth of Feminine Satanism."

Naglowska's staunch disciples, mostly budding intellectuals and poets, renovated a vacant studio room in Montparnasse. They decorated the walls of the Golden Arrow temple with mirrors and charts that depicted "the ternary progress of humanity" and the beatific consummation that resulted from detached and "ego-free" intercourse. In that *umbilicus mundi,* the tiny prophetess perched on a wooden armchair while a half-dozen naked couples shifted from a succession of Kama Sutra-like embraces to unite into the "Rite of the Square," a human "magical chain."

The converts' fraternal status — "Sweepers of the Court," "Liberated Hunters," or "Invincible Warriors" — was determined by their mastery of the TTT beliefs and participation in the sacred work. Each matriculation, or Satanic Mystery, was increasingly more challenging and arduous. The otherworldly revelations

unfolded in three rungs: the "Mass of Gold," the "Illumination of Sex," and, ultimately, the "Mystery of Hanging."

The Mass of Gold was, for the most part, a solemn occasion with few moving parts: a prayer over silver chalices of wine, trance communication with Lucifer and Satan, a choral interlude, oaths of allegiance, Eurhythmic dance, and the washing of the postulants' feet. This preliminary rite was deferential, precise, and controlled.

The Mystery of Hanging was another matter and sometimes a cause for concern. In the last part of the convocation, *Sophiales* (seventeen-year-old female acolytes) lined up before a row of naked inductees. The girls gently stroked the men's penises until they were engorged and fully erect. The Invincible Warriors then stepped on chairs and placed nooses over their necks. They leaped forward in order to asphyxiate themselves. Once they passed out, the cords around their throats were released and the men fell to the floor. On command, the scrum of *initiatrices* mounted the supine and semi-conscious Warriors to make sweet nurturing love to them.

In follow-up sessions, both the male supplicants and female accomplices claimed that they experienced an ecstatic jolt of "unspeakable happiness." (In August 1934, *Paris Magazine* prattled in their joke section that the unadventurous cultists had discovered only forty-three ways to dangle themselves into orgasm.)

At the beginning of 1936, Naglowska called an emergency meeting of her most trusted advisers and sycophants. A year previously, she had predicted a great catastrophe was on the horizon, "the War of 1936." Now the fifty-two-year-old High Priestess of Love announced that she consulted her prized magic mirror and saw an image of her impending doom. It was time for her to close shop and return to Switzerland.

ABOVE LEFT: A chalice placed on the Priestess

ABOVE CENTER: Stéphane Pisella, *Maria de Naglowska Begins the Mass of Gold*, 1935

BELOW: R. Leflers, *Hanged Man*, 1935

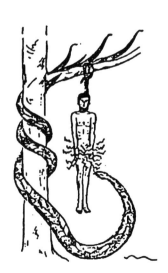

ABOVE: Louis Berthommé-St. André, *The Hanging*, 1935

RIGHT: Naglowska holds court at *la Coupole* after the Mass of Gold, 1935

Some speculated there might have been an emphatically less supernatural motive for the sorceress' abrupt decision: maybe an Invincible Warrior lethally expired from asphyxiation and the matter needed to be concealed. It was impossible to know but her divination proved accurate. Four months later in Zurich, Naglowska died in bed by her daughter's side.

WILLIAM SEABROOK, THE AMERICAN *BOKOR*

A *New York Times* reporter, feature writer for Hearst International, and author of five travelogues, William Seabrook (1886–1945) popularized the first-person investigation of exotic customs in remote regions, their manifestations in the civilized world, and the explorers of the occult. He was also a frank sadist, obsessed with bondage and cannibalism. These maniacal enthusiasms constantly intertwined, even if Seabrook had to alter facts in order to drop them into the same narrative.

Seabrook, a volunteer in the American Field Service of the French Army, received the *Croix de Guerre* for his service at Verdun. During the twenties, the peripatetic amateur traversed Turkey, Lebanon, Syria, and parts of Arabia and Iraq. Seabrook's specialty was bringing the reader into his backwater escapades — far-flung pockets where devil-worshippers, hirsute tribal chieftains, whirling dervishes, desert vampires, wonderworkers, and white-slavers lurked. The episodic nature of his *Adventures in Arabia* with its melodramatic breaks already read like a radio serial script.

Seabrook's next book, *The Magic Island*, brought the swashbuckling writer to the attention of a broader and more anxious public in 1929. It was the first mass-market account of Haiti's indigenous folk religion, Voodoo. Willie described in ghastly detail its animal sacrifices and hex dolls; its soul-exchanging trance dances; and, most disturbing, Voodoo's black-magic *bokors*, shamans who could "change the skins" of their adversaries or revive legions of the undead. In fact, it was here that America learned about the existence of *zombis*. And *Magic Island*, translated into a cornucopia of languages, itself was a kind of zombie, never going out of print, devouring the imaginations of future anthropologists, and shuffling its way into every medium.

In 1930, with his future wife in tow, Seabrook backtracked to Paris. He declared France the contemporary hub of European witchcraft. At the Orly customs desk, Willie was asked to empty out his luggage. Handcuffs, whips, chains, and other S&M paraphernalia spilled over the counter. The French inspector deduced that these were the accessories of an American gangster. Seabrook corrected the official: he was no mob heavy, merely a practicing sadist, one of the admirers of the Marquis de Sade. The bemused administer flashed a broad smile and waved the nomadic iconoclast through the airport gate.

Fellow American journalists in Paris thrilled to Willie's forays into occult Paris. Seabrook told George Seldes, the international correspondent for the *Chicago Tribune,* that he joined a Black Mass church, which met in a Montmartre cellar. The group was an interracial crew; still the naked altar sacrifice had to be pearly white. Some traditions were inviolable. Once the fiendish worshippers offered him a cooked stew of human remains. Seabrook kept it to himself at the time but later complained that the arm and rump tasted like coarse, under-seasoned veal.

STUDIO
DELAMBRE
1932

Another *Trib* reporter, Wambly Bald, attempted to infatuate Seabrook with tales of Naglowska's Brotherhood. It seemed right up Willie's perverse alley. Unfortunately, there is no evidence that either bothered to attend her temple services.

According to Marjorie Worthington, Seabrook's put-upon mate and struggling novelist, "Lovemaking, for Willie, was a complicated process, all mixed up with his complexes, fetishes, and compulsions." He once took her to the selection parlor at the Aux Belles Poules. Naturally, the jaded adventurer found no reason to stay. His sexual aesthetics veered in more unconventional directions.

Two incidents at their apartment in the Rive Gauche stuck in Marjorie's mental craw for decades. Both occurred in 1932, shortly after the Seabrooks returned from an expedition to the French Sudan. (This voyage would prompt yet another questionable book.)

Willie decided to throw a lavish pre-luncheon party for his French benefactors and other assorted "stuffed shirts." The buccaneer of the bizarre decided to show-case one of his "complexes." In a corner of their flat, Marjorie spotted a peculiar sight: "There, hanging by her wrists from a chain, was Mimi, one of those call girls of Montparnasse, who would do almost anything for money. [...] She was naked from the waist up, and her bare toes just touched the floor." As they filed in, the guests greeted their American hosts and averted their eyes from the bound and gagged Mimi. The French sophisticates sipped *apéritifs* and engaged in polite conversation before they accompanied Seabrook to their restaurant repast. As soon as the society bunch exited, Marjorie unchained the suspended *marcheuse* and handed her a stiff drink.

The second occasion took place a few months later. Seabrook invited Man Ray, the Surrealist photographer, and his partner, Lee Miller, to their duplex. Again there was a prostitute strung to the staircase. This time, two other fetish-clad *femmes* were also engaged. Willie wanted to capture a more intense S&M *mise-en-scène* on film.

Man Ray scholars claim this unusual photo shoot as an uncredited project in his vast body of work. Yet there is no proof that the acclaimed artist personally snapped the pictures. (His biographers even remain vague over its date in his *oeuvre*.) Ray photographed several fetishist portraits in his studio but none resembled these nor did they relate to his sexual interests.

A simpler and more logical explanation was that this weird series had a different dramaturge: it was created and filmed by Seabrook himself; Ray likely provided the equipment and technical assistance. This would account for the fact that Marjorie never referenced Man's input, Seabrook did not appear in any of the photographs, or why Ray, throughout his career, never acknowledged their existence.

That evening of torturous fantasy was Seabrook's last recorded erotic venture in Paris. The next year, he left France and began treatment for his acute alcoholism. Seabrook continued to write about French werewolfism and murderous "leopard women" until 1945, when he swallowed a bottle of sleeping pills. The county coroner in upstate New York declared Willie's death a suicide. ❦

HITLER'S BROTHEL AND LIBÉRATION

I'm almost ashamed to say it, but I've never had so much fun in my life. Those nights during the Occupation were fantastic.

— Fabienne Jamet, *One Two Two*, 1975 —

My heart is French but my ass is international.

— Arlette, explaining her relationship with a Luftwaffe captain, 1944 —

IN THE EYES OF MANY, the image of Paris in World War II was always that of a Frenchwoman: the eager schoolgirl assisting a bashful squad of foreign liberators; the stockinged carrier of contagion who preyed on the loneliness of Wehrmacht infantrymen; the wide-eyed lass held captive and ravished by the very same troops; the self-sacrificing Resistance heroine; the victorious Marianne symbol with pinup arms stretched to heaven; the comely twenty-something wildly kissing a Yank in the backseat of a jeep; the shorn and naked "horizontal collaborator," paraded down into the city square; and, yet again, the rapacious vixen, who preferred Champagne and cheap perfume over a morning basin of hot water and soap.

OPPOSITE: German soldiers at the *Bal Tarabin*, 1942

THE OCCUPATION

From the beginning of the Occupation in June 1940, it was clear that Paris was to be treated like no other conquered city in the expanding Nazi Reich. The citizens of Paris, it was thought, could be cajoled, sweet-talked, or rationally swayed to support the Hitlerian cause for a prosperous and racially reordered New Europe. Unlike the Danes, Norwegians, and Dutch, many Frenchmen long voiced fears of cultural, economic, or genetic contamination from the Jews and Slavs, who imbedded themselves so deeply inside their beloved fatherland.

Yet like anxious couples on a blind date, both the German administrators from the Foreign Office, Gestapo, and Wehrmacht and the Parisians under their command

were at various moments cooperative, apprehensive, charmed, incredulous, or repelled. It all depended on individual perceptions and constantly changing external circumstances — the success of military operations outside France; the levels of passive or active resistance in the city and its suburbs; severity of rationing, appropriation of property and goods, and forced labor; divergent edicts issued in Berlin; strikes or threats of them in essential services and munitions factories; expectations of an Allied victory; treatment of French minorities; and German attitudes toward French authority and their cultural proclivities. Of course, the Nazi authorities subdivided the civilian population into endless categories: some favored by the conquerors for a host of reasons, others ignored or subjected to brutal decrees.

It was no easy task ruling Paris or dealing with Nazis.

To be sure, misery and deprivation in Occupied France was not a universal condition. Some Parisians made fortunes in *le marché noir* or working directly with the Germans. Those in the entertainment and sex industries — the Germans usually

couldn't tell them apart — raked in bundles of Vichy *francs*. Again, this twisted and thorny exchange, which looked shameful to those on the sidelines, had many reciprocal benefits.

WEHRMACHT AMUSEMENTS

Britain and France declared war on Germany in September 1939 but there was little combat until the following spring when Wehrmacht armies bounded around France's impregnable fortifications on the eastern border. This in-between period was nicknamed the "phony war" because, while the Allied governments began general mobilization and other military preparations, the warring states had yet to engage along the contested Maginot Line.

In Paris, all commercial amusements were forcibly closed. Cabarets, music-halls, *dancings*, and theatre houses — even the *maisons de tolérance* — fell into a financial tailspin. In the midst of the Great War, they were thought to be vital morale-boosters; in 1939 they were considered unpatriotic diversions. Around Christmastime, the French public tired of these civil constraints and the evening curfews were gradually eased. Montmartre revived, if in a weakened state.

Ironically, what saved Paris' tourist and performing arts venues from out-and-out collapse was the German invasion. Suddenly Wehrmacht soldiers and Nazi administers by the tens of thousands flooded the City of Pleasure. They packed the revue houses, nightclubs, cabarets, and best restaurants. And these occupiers were free with their money and proved to be less discriminating than the Anglo-Saxons.

The Nazi cultural czars, who promoted High German art within the Reich and the *Volksdeutsche* communities outside it, were stymied when it came to Paris. Bach, Wagner, and Strauss were given the philharmonic treatment in German-commandeered amphitheatres. Nazi propaganda film features and newsreels played in soldiers' cinemas and movie houses. But this was no Warsaw or Oslo. The decadence of *la Ville-Lumière* had to be approached with caution.

TOP: Casino de Paris, *Loves of Paris*, 1941

Many German politicos in the military thought of the city, once emptied of Jews, as a permanent recreational haven for their brave guardians. It was far from the virtuous motherland and a place for manly comforts. Besides the forty-five naked revues offered every night, there were nearly one hundred shops for intimate apparel and perfume. Even with the rationing of meat and other luxury food items, Parisian restaurants and bistros still offered better *prix fixes* than one could find in Berlin.

The Teutonic enthusiasm for Parisian culture took many unexpected turns. Legitimate theatre productions — both boulevard comedies and poetic dramas — could now survive the critical onslaught from local reviewers. No matter what the supercilious first-nighters thought, live stage shows were overbooked — usually by the attentive *Fritzes*. Flops that would have closed after the first negative notices continued for weeks.

For instance, Jean-Paul Sartre's Existentialist play *The Flies*, a 1943 wakeup call about freedom and power in mythic Argos, overflowed with cordial German spectators. Nazi censors saw no reason to curtail the philosophical discourse. A functioning occupation in France needed to display its own *savoir-faire* and acceptance of such toothless prewar conventions as symbolic protest theatre.

Jazz, banned in the Reich itself, never deserted the nocturnal metropolis. Chez Florence was a spellbinding Wehrmacht destination during the first year of German occupation. In June 1941, it was shuttered along with the other showcases of American and colonial "negrification." Predictably, the irrepressible soundsmiths from America's segregated Chitlin Circuit re-emerged in the dimly lit back rows of the up-to-the-minute French and Gypsy nightclubs.

The 1942 film *Mademoiselle Swing* relocated the youthful American import squarely onto the pale old Continent; Negros weren't even necessary for the airing of African-American music. The Gypsy guitarist and inventor of "hot jazz" fusion, Django Reinhardt abandoned his family in London and returned to Nazi Paris where he remounted his original jazz Quintet with four Africans and a Jew.

Despite his ethnic background and degenerate musical style, the outlier Reinhardt thrived unimpeded by the Vichy *Sûreté*. He performed in the major nightclubs and cabarets under the protection of a Luftwaffe *Oberleutnant*, Dietrich Schulz-Köhn. The German officer relished his *nom de guerre*, "Doktor Jazz."

PROSTITUTION

Prostitution, one of the many plagues that Hitler attributed to modern Jewry in *Mein Kampf*, had been pretty much swept from the German heartland in 1933. A mere seven years later, commercialized sex flourished throughout occupied Paris. An estimated 100,000 *occasionnalles* worked the streets and cafés of the city — a five hundred percent increase from before the war. And the *filles de joie* gravitated toward the alien hordes for more than basic sustenance; they seemed to wholeheartedly treasure the company of the *boches*.

Marie-Thérèse Cointré recalled, "The Germans were often handsome kids, good-natured, and lots of fun. I had a pretty good time with them. I think I always preferred blond men. Because of their skin, I guess. […] There was the uniform and the language I didn't understand very well. That meant you could imagine things. I liked that. They had a mixture of shyness and roughness."

To the French, the Nordic men-at-arms were breathtaking and exotically sexual. With their luminescent hair and strange manners, quintessential primitiveness and erotic style of dress, the Nazi troops on leave were the newest Joséphine Bakers. And lovelorn Parisiennes began to dye their tresses Gypsy black in an attempt to emphasize their own sirenly Mediterranean allure.

The magnetic draw was mutual except in one regard: the Germans were repulsed and terrified by French notions of hygiene. The girls did not wash; at least, not according to Aryan standards. They rinsed their vaginas in bidets and splashed perfume and powder over their sweaty skin. In fact, the *fromage* connoisseurs deemed the mixed scent of female perspiration and bottled fragrance

TOP: German officers at the *Bal Tarabin*, 1942

ABOVE: *Les Canova*, 1940

OCCUPATION/LIBÉRATION SLANG

COLLABOS: Vichy henchmen or collaborators.

EMBOCHIES: French girls and women who were accused of sleeping with German soldiers.

ÉPURATION LÉGALE: The Free French tribunals that determined the guilt or innocence of people accused of wartime collaboration.

FEMMES TONDUES ("Shorn Women"): During the Purge, *embochies* who were publicly humiliated by having their heads shaved.

FRITZES: Germans. [Variant name: *Boches*.]

GESTAPACHES: Thugs who worked with the Germans during the Occupation. [Comic neologism combining Gestapo with Apaches.]

GESTAPETTES: Homosexual collaborators or collabos. [Comic neologism combining Gestapo and Tapettes.]

MARCHÉ NOIR: Black market.

ZAZOUS: Hip youngsters, who telegraphed their social nonchalance through their jazzy getups: men with sunglasses and long checkered jackets; women in short skirts and striped stockings.

ZIGZAG: Intercourse. [GI neologism.]

ABOVE: Lulu, the Shy Poule, 1941

an aphrodisiac attractant. An overly scrubbed and disinfected body lacked the necessary pheromones for proper Gallic courtship.

Squads of Wehrmacht medical teams erected venereal clinics across Paris, posted austere German-language warnings on Montmartre walls, and issued VD inspection cards to every variety of prostitute. The fifteen Sanitation Officers who monitored the physical examinations were themselves subject to intense supervision. Any negligence on their part was considered "an act of sabotage."

Twenty *maisons closes* were requisitioned for German officers, German enlisted men and noncombatants, or for Vichyites and recognized collaborators. The remaining two hundred brothels were open to the run-of-the-mill Pierres. (Wehrmacht statisticians estimated that the sex industry utilized more than six thousand rooms.) The Vichy government imposed special taxes on all of the shuttered houses. No owners complained. It was a booming *bisnesse* with a contented clientele.

Many German officers regarded the designated *maisons de tolérance* as their private domiciles. These were convivial environments, where they could relax with their comrades and the madams, share bottles of Champagne, and dance with the dolled-up *femmes*. In 1940 and 1941, Germans routinely brought flowers and boxes of chocolates to the brothels. And one always knew when Hermann Goering frequented the Chab: his SS security patrol, cradling submachine guns, stood guard by the stony entrance.

A few of the luxury *maisons closes* operated outside the parameters of the restrictive Nazi decrees; these were neutral zones, where German bureaucrats and military men, in civilian dress, could intermingle with Paris' elite. One such establishment, *L'Étoile de Kléber,* opened its doors in 1941 and was known for its superb cuisine and artistic clientele. Édith Piaf lived on de Kléber's top floor and entertained her fellow revue stars, notably Chevalier and Miss, in the dining hall. A few blocks from the Arc de Triomphe, it was also a favorite haunt for both French auxiliary agents in the employ of the Gestapo and Resistance commanders.

One night, plainclothes German detectives raided the place in a citywide hunt for unregistered Jews. They rounded up the French guests and directed them to drop their trousers in order to scrutinize their penises. The outraged customers vehemently refused to comply with the humiliating inspection, except for Cocteau. He proudly exposed his uncircumcised member to the undercover cops.

In 1975, Fabienne Jamet, the madam of the 122, published her memoirs and gave a string of television interviews about her wartime experiences. These sunny recollections about the Occupation and her provocative attitude dumbfounded contemporary French historians. For Jamet, it was a golden era, the most profitable in her brothel's long and celebrated history.

During of the Battle of Britain, squadrons of Luftwaffe pilots spent last nights at The One before engaging in their perilous missions. Once, after a late-afternoon frolic, Fabienne's girls played the British music-hall standard and Royal Air Force anthem "It's a Long Way to Tipperary" on the *maison's* gramophone. The Luftwaffe airmen followed the prostitutes' lead and sang the patriotic English lyrics in perfect harmony. It was typical of Jamet's comical reminiscences. And when the aerial combat over London exacted significant German losses, the gloomy Luftwaffe boys shared their amphetamine rations with Le One's employees in one final reckless and sleepless shindig.

Ernst Radecker, head of German counterintelligence, was a regular client at Fabienne's spic-and-span palace and brought along a few visiting Berlin bigwigs.

ABOVE TOP: German officers in brothel

ABOVE CENTER: Venereal certificate for Le Grand 4, 1944

ABOVE BOTTOM: *La Chabanais* in the German brochure, *Das Bordellwesen in Paris*, 1940

But there were internal problems. All of Paris' warring factions — Nazi officers, *gestapaches*, Corsican gangsters from Montmartre, and Resistance fighters — spent their nights at the 122 and, instead of choosing bedroom partners in the Garden selection lounge, they would sometimes draw pistols on their inebriated opponents. Eventually Jamet placed them into separate quarters. And she required all firearms to be deposited in The One's foyer. Even this simple precaution proved inadequate. A few of her customers snuck in grenades and juggled them in shows of derring-do.

Just before his departure in 1944, a German captain warned Jamet that she would soon pine for her Axist benefactors; the backwoods American GIs would display little reverence for her august enterprise. Jamet shrugged it off but, within a few months, she had to concur with his uncanny prediction.

Fortunately for Fabienne, in December, during the Gaullist inquiry over her collaboration, Resistance leaders unexpectedly revealed that she had been one of Paris' most generous contributors to their cause. An amicable profiteer, made wealthy off *boche* lust, and a clandestine funder of the besieged French underground, Jamet could be seen as a tainted symbol of the pleasure capital under foreign domination.

BELOW: Suzy Carrier, *The Cyclist*, 1941

HOME FRONT

Marshal Philippe Pétain, Vichy France's eighty-four-year-old Chief of State, attempted to reconcile the needs of his vanquished nation to a cascade of Nazi demands. Mimicking Hitler, he declared a countrywide regeneration based on "Work, Family, and Patriotism." The police, civil service, press and radio, labor unions, political parties, mercantile associations, financial and education systems were all reorganized into the Fascist mold. Pétain's totalitarian blueprint of National Revolution supplanted the democratic Third Republic. But, in the end, everything was subject to German approval or military exigencies.

During the four Black Years, the majority of Parisians were acquiescent, trying to gauge the political temperature if they could and outguess their neighbors' plans for survival. It was a time to hunker down and figure out the next strategic move for the week or month. Among the most desperate were the wives of the two million French soldiers incarcerated in German POW camps. For them, sex was another black-market exchange that could advance their careers or put food on the table.

Making love with strangers or in unlikely abodes surfaced as a therapeutic means of shattering the malaise of the defeat. Many Parisians found anonymous companionship and comfort in the movie theatres and catacombs. The French birth rate shot up in those years. Some saw this subterranean activity as yet another form of Gallic defiance.

Even *chanteuses* and starlets expressed their contempt for the invader with sultry disdain; they openly socialized in captivating outfits as if the war were a temporary impediment to their city's more elevated callings. Social events, like the autumn Longchamp Races remained *de rigueur* occasions for fashion plates and their aristocratic admirers. Naturally, dashing Nazi commandants were not far behind either. Female icons like Colette, Miss, Coco Chanel, and Arletty, the prewar film titillation and lead in Marcel Carné's *Les Enfants du Paradis*, allowed themselves to be "occupied" by the "handsome as gods" German officers.

France's foremost artists, journalists, and intellectuals proved to be surprisingly compliant to the New Order. Exhibitions, floor shows, gallery openings, and salon teas continued in tasteful chic-chic fashion. In *The Republic of Silence*, Sartre recalled the strange and liberating experience of living under Nazi repression: "We were never more free than under the German occupation." Every thought, every gesture, every drink, every debauched soirée could be seen as an act of protest. His partner Simone de Beauvoir went even further. According to Patrick Buisson, she wrote about the "spontaneous friendliness" of the Germans and their physical vigor, which included near-naked gymnastic exercise in public squares.

In forties Hollywood and in the popular American press, the brutal domination of France and its citizens' cunning disobedience was a durable and emotionally satisfying theme. Nazi tyranny and resistance in other defeated countries had less staying power. For one, it meant dealing with the subjugation of the Jews, a forbidden topic. Also, in the American mindscape, Paris — or any French town — was populated with a surfeit of female stunners in black berets and tight blouses. And, like malevolent automatons, the cowardly Aryan bullyboys and monocled

ABOVE LEFT: Arletty in the film *Daybreak*, 1939

ABOVE RIGHT: André Zucca, *Rose Valois, Mme. Le Monnier, and Agnès Capri at the Longchamp Race Track*, 1943

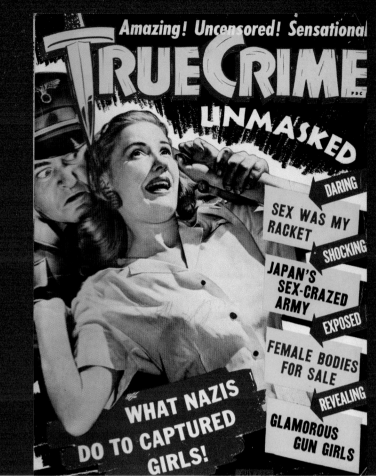

perverts seemed programmed to sexually menace any sweet-faced detainee. But before anything worse could happen, downed American or RAF pilots always came to the rescue.

Well, at least one-half of the wartime melodramatic equation was spot on: in a world of scarcity, Frenchwomen found ingenious ways to project style and glamour. On the other hand, there was little incentive for German officers to manhandle or rape innocent Parisiennes. (What torments happened in the Gestapo interrogation pens, of course, was another story.)

Historically, forcible sex by the blond barbarians in the streets of Paris before 1944 was uncommon. That kind of behavior was reserved for the Eastern front. And too many French girls had already thrown in their lot with the enemy. They even had a name: *embochies*.

FORBIDDEN PARIS

Parisians lived in an improbable erotic bubble. Inside Nazidom, there were few places where "wild prostitution" and extensive black-market trade were tolerated or categorically ignored. This was also true for homosexuality. While German gays were hunted and hauled off to concentration camps in their homeland, queer venues in Paris remained open for business as they had before the war. (The Jewish-owned or operated clubs, of course, changed hands.) More curious still, the gay and lesbian cabarets that advertised in Wehrmacht guidebooks nearly doubled in size during the Occupation. German troops at leave could not get enough of the forbidden theatrics. It was something to daydream about while writing sedately jingoistic letters to family and friends.

And, other than being amusing forums for high-minded perversity, lesbian and gay nightclubs held a secondary attraction. They were ideal fronts for all manner of illicit activity. In Liberty's and the Colisée's underground club, *gestapettes* and black-marketers used the toilets and greenrooms for weekly contacts with their German suppliers. The smutty atmospherics fostered petty outlaw behavior that enveloped even the most resolute Nazi supermen.

In Montparnasse, Solidor's lesbian cabaret La Vie Parisienne was so inundated with Master Race tourists that her detractors labeled it "La Vie Hitlérienne." Suzy brought the uniformed spectators to their feet when she sang "Lili Marlene" in French or belted out her saucy Fascist salute, "The Thirty-First of August." Its comic refrain was "So shit on the Queen of England/Who declared war on us." And, by shacking up with a German officer, the Breton-born mermaid appeared to jettison not only national pride but her devoted queer coterie in one fell swoop.

Gay men, like adolescent Parisiennes, were thunderstruck by the German soldiers' chiseled appearance. Not only were the conquerors tall and flaxen-haired, they came marching in shiny boots, leather trim, and burnished metal. Young male prostitutes found enthusiastic Wehrmacht clients in the *pissoirs* and bathhouses throughout the city. This manly aspect of sexual collaboration had immediate repercussions.

In 1942, Marshal Pétain amended the Napoleonic Penal Code to redefine the legal boundary between "natural" (heterosexual) and "unnatural" (gay) sexual acts with minors. Homosexual seduction of underage boys was now subject to fines and prison terms, ranging from six months to three years. State criminalization of this "shameless" same-sex corruption remained on the books long after the war.

Yet queer desire was difficult to tamp down in Vichy France. Pétain's Minister of Education, Abel Bonnard,

LE MONOCLE 60, Bd Edgar-Quinet
(U-Bahn Edgar-Quinet)

Das eleganteste Kabaret im Montparnasse

DAS BERÜHMTE ORCHESTER

SEINE LUSTIGEN SÄNGERINNEN und TÄNZERINNEN

GEÖFFNET BIS 5 Uhr MORGENS

Fernspr. DANton 41-30

SUZY SOLIDOR
SINGT IHRE MARINE - LIEDER
und stellt vor den unvergleichlichen Komiker

HENRY BRY

MONA GOYA
die französische Filmschauspielerin die schon oft in Berlin filmte
UND

CHRISTIANE NÉRÉ
MIT IHREM FEINEN PARISER HUMOR
u. s. w. IM KABARET

LA VIE PARISIENNE
12, rue Ste-ANNE - Tél. RIC. 97-86
(Av. de l'Opéra - gegenüber U-bahn " Pyramides ")

a former travel writer, was an acknowledged pedophile with an inclination for teenage German troopers. The old general once groused to his cabinet, "It is scandalous to entrust the young to that *tapette!*" But the *bon vivant* Bonnard remained at his post until Pétain's government joined the retreating Wehrmacht armies into a hurried German exile.

GAY *COLLABOS*

From the Occupation's earliest days, the Germans realized that they needed a vast pool of French sympathizers to adequately police the semi-autonomous motherland. Generally, Nazi authorities eschewed Paris' homegrown Fascists and nationalists. Foreign-born gangsters often proved to be obedient lackeys and suitably ruthless. In a curious twist, a few French lesbians and gay men were also appointed to positions of power in 1940. Among the most notorious Vichy *collabos* was a pair of misfit homosexuals, Violette Morris and Maurice Sachs.

Sometimes known as "Fat Claude" and a frequent patron of Le Fétiche and Monocle cabarets, the cross-dressing Morris (1893–1944) was commonly featured as France's prominent Sapphic public figure. Between the wars, her athletic prowess became legendary. Morris excelled at field sports, boxing and Greco-Roman wrestling, weight lifting, water polo, archery, and tennis as well as competitive racing in horseback riding, bicycling, motorcycling, stock cars, and airplanes.

Although banned from the French Women's Athletic Federation because of her over-the-top lesbian lifestyle, Morris nonetheless supplied Parisian gossip columnists with an endless stream of sensational *faits divers*. In 1928, her female lover revealed that she terminated their relationship because Violette had undergone an elective double mastectomy. Reportedly, the champion driver had submitted to the voluntary surgery in order to fit inside the cockpit of her specially designed racecar.

In 1936, Morris received a personal invitation from Hitler to attend the Berlin Summer Olympics. Recruited as an undercover operative for the Nazi SS, Morris

delivered precise information about the locations of France's Maginot Line, hidden defensive positions around Paris, and schematic blueprints of the army's vaunted *Somua* S35 tank.

Once the Germans established a smoothly functioning regime, Violette took on a new role: to work cheek-by-jowl with the Gestapo in ferreting out British SOE (Special Operations Executive) couriers that were scattered about the city and to oversee the interrogations of female Resistance fighters. Morris' procedures were described as especially sadistic. The so-called "Hyena of Avenue Foch" wielded a nail-studded whip and devised other abysmal means of torture.

The Gaullist Government-in-Exile sentenced the vicious *gousse* to death *in absentia*. A joint team of British and Free French commandos trapped Morris on a country road in 1944. They peppered her supercharged sedan with machine gun fire, killing the arch-*gestapette* and her lesbian compatriots, in a Bonnie-and-Clyde-like shootout.

Born to a Jewish family of jewelers in Paris, Maurice Sachs (1906–1945) converted to Catholicism when he was nineteen. The young author, with a penchant for occult themes, had befriended Cocteau and Coco Chanel. A difficult personality and a probable kleptomaniac, Sachs savagely turned on his mentors after being charged with petty theft. Like others of his ilk, Maurice was torn between a lifelong desire to join the priesthood or bandy around the beaches to search of homosexual companionship. Drafted in 1939, the conflicted novelist was soon cashiered out of the army for sexual misconduct.

In the first years of the Occupation, Sachs helped smuggle wealthy Jewish families into France's Unoccupied Zone in the South. When that became too dangerous, despite its lucrative rewards, he fell in with the Gestapo. As a Jewish informant and well-regarded writer, Sachs provided German intelligence with a unique perspective on the private machinations of Paris' artistic inner circles.

Before the Wehrmacht withdrawal, however, the wily Semitic interloper was dispatched to a concentration camp near Hamburg. At Fuhlsbüttel, French inmates uncovered Sachs' previous Nazi associations, strangled him during a barracks melee, and tossed his body to the camp's guard dogs.

LIBÉRATION

Once the Allied armies secured a foothold in Normandy in early June 1944, most Parisians and their German overlords realized that the days of Nazi rule were strictly numbered. Armed Resistance activity intensified and tens of thousands of Frenchmen suddenly found their way into underground *Maquis* cells. Besides blowing up railroad tracks and attacking German garrison trains, the French Forces of the Interior (FFI) began their campaign to exact revenge on native collaborators.

For General de Gaulle, this was primarily a political moment. The French uprisings that preceded Eisenhower's unsteady offensive had little social cohesion. Despite a common enemy, his *Fifi* squads were practically at war with themselves. They splintered politically across the old prewar spectrum: Communist

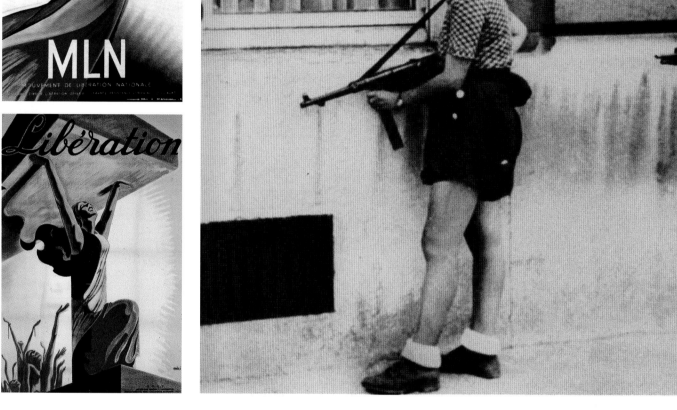

ABOVE: Movement de Libération Nationale and Phili, *Marianne*, 1944

RIGHT: *One Step Forward, One Step Back*, 1944

cadres, anti-Franco Spanish Republicans and Syndicalists, Socialists, right-wing Nationalists, and French democrats. Even de Gaulle's frontline battalions, the Army of Liberation, were comprised of mixed units of French soldiers and dark-skinned colonials. Yet, the self-declared Prime Minister was determined to see the emancipation of Paris as a penultimate victory achieved by combat-hardened, indigenous heroes.

Five days before General Patton's Third Army captured Paris on August 24th, 1944, *Fifi* irregulars began their long-awaited revolt. They barricaded streets and firebombed the stalled lines of German half-tracks and fuel trucks. The stop-start fighting and sniping went on for several days until de Gaulle's all-white 2nd Armored Division swept into the city from the West. Twenty-four hours later, the German Military Governor, who defied Hitler's directive to blast the city into "utter ruins," formally surrendered.

On August 29th, the French and American armies celebrated their joint triumph on the Champs-Élysées with long columns of tanks and a procession of marching bands. *Vogue*-inspired posters of Marianne were quickly plastered around Paris. *Libération* and real sovereignty had finally come to *la Ville-Lumière*.

THE PURGE

Civic efforts to reestablish French authority in the newly liberated towns and cities were often haphazard and chaotic. There was precious little consensus in most municipalities. The Black Years had contaminated all the traditional legislative structures. And, to a large degree, the overthrow of German-appointed councils resulted in orgies of communal retribution.

L'Épuration, or the Purge, followed in the path of advancing Allied divisions. Unrecorded numbers of officials and collaborators were assassinated by the *Fifis* or shunted off to detention centers. Shockingly, the most widely publicized punishments were reserved for the *embochies*, the girls and women who slept with German soldiers.

In 1944, over twenty thousand Frenchwomen were tried and condemned as "horizontal collaborators." Once identified by *Maquis* witnesses, they were gathered in outdoor arenas, subjected to taunts by jeering crowds, and stripped naked. As a matter of course, local prefects force-marched the petrified women down main streets onto the steps of city hall. There, on raised platforms, the *embochies'* hair was sheared and swastikas painted across their foreheads. In some cases, the accused sex traitors were anally abused with broomsticks.

ABOVE: Roland Forgues, *Libération de Paris* paper cutout, 1944

ABOVE: The haircut and marking, 1944

RIGHT: The traitors' promenade, 1944; *I Caused My Husband to be Shot*, 1944

To foreign observers, especially American photojournalists, these seemed to be baffling displays of Medieval-like savagery. After all, no turncoat males in France were ever treated in such a humiliating manner; even the homosexual partners of German soldiers were largely ignored and spared the postwar, score-settling fury. If anything, photographs of the wretched nudes prefigured other searing images that would be posted from occupied Europe — those of emaciated survivors in German-run labor and death camps.

In the first weeks of *Libération, s*hame and remorse for the French defeat and acquiescence to Hun control had been deflected onto a few thousand civilian women. Their bodies symbolized Gallic weakness and national betrayal. Buisson described this psycho-political motive as "the revenge of the French male." Its disquieting impulse would reshape the country's erotic future.

GI PARADISE

FDR's Hollywood had pitched a captivating vision of French womanhood: young or postmenstrual, they were a sorority of indomitable, saucy creatures. It was a useful propaganda ploy and GIs, naturally, subscribed to the arresting fantasy. Pushing the Wehrmacht out of Italy or the Low Countries meant one thing, but unshackling

French families from Nazi bonds brought more corporal rewards. The U.S. Army even issued translation sheets that assisted the grunts in finding their way into Gallic hearts and boudoirs.

Unlike the disciplined German troops, most Yanks had little patience with French folkways. Hardly any spoke the language or cared to learn it and they were often violent. As many local entrepreneurs quickly discovered, the American liberators appeared to be from another world or civilization entirely. Scrums of off-duty U.S. infantrymen commonly engaged in petty theft, gang rape, fisticuffs, and wanton destruction of property. French constables had never seen anything like it. (Of the hundreds of GIs charged with sexual assault by the American Military Police in France, twenty-nine were publicly hanged, nearly 90% being Colored support troops.)

Even sober GIs on leave had difficulty in distinguishing which *femmes* were innocent flirts, flashing patriotic smiles, and which were bona fide beddable *cocottes*. The soldiers' stammering uncertainties replicated the comic confusion of previous Anglo-Saxon tourists. Hand gestures quickly became the lingua franca of the French sex trade. Eventually, a bilingual term, *zigzag*, was coined for fucking. It rolled off the tongue with an unmistakable implication.

Better than paper currency, the Americans possessed edible goods and nylon stockings. Their K-ration kits could feed a horde of street urchins. And every GI within jeep range of a PX had access to the "Four Cs": cigarettes, Coca-Cola, chewing gum, and chocolates. A pack of Luckies could easily be bartered for one *zigzag*. To the French, blonde American cigarettes were an exotic novelty. And at fifty cents to a few dollars per carton, any lowly private could purchase an erotic repast for a palmful of copper pennies.

In Paris, the *maisons closes* readied themselves for the newest invaders. Strangely, the most American-styled brothel, Le Sphinx, was declared off-limits for GIs. Many of the *maisons de rendez-vous,* in keeping with the U.S. Army racial policies, restricted their clientele to whites or Negros only. The larger houses maintained segregated entrances and parlors. No self-righteous hillbilly wanted his pecker within thrusting range of "a jigaboo's beef bayonet."

At the 122, around-the-clock madness reigned. Starting at 10 a.m., mobs of

Present arms
Portez armes

TOP: *A G.I. Tries His Luck,* 1945

ABOVE LEFT: Doudou, *Present Arms,* 1945

ABOVE RIGHT: United States Army handbill, 1944

CONVERSATION
The G. I. and the French Girl

ABOVE: *Mad*, "Whaa? Me Black?" 1947

BELOW LEFT: *Paris-Spectacles* (December 6, 1944)

BELOW RIGHT: *Joséphine Baker Back in Paris*, 1944 (From the JC Garrett Collection)

unruly American soldiers filled the foyer. Still drunk from their evening of carousing, some of the hell-raisers continued their spree, sipping from bottles of perfume and eau de Cologne. Unable to climax, the poisoned warriors blamed the *fournisseurs* and attempted to asphyxiate them.

The first Americans at the One shot up the Japanese lounge. They claimed it was their brotherly contribution to the Pacific War. Another group of inebriated Southerners almost lynched one of Jamet's African girls. The shaken *fille de maison* described her attackers as crazed maniacs, possibly escaped convicts from Sing-Sing. Worse still, a machine-gun-toting GI ran down into the 122 kitchen in search of boiled corn. The poor battle-weary vet obviously had a hankering for some down-home cuisine.

The *maisons d'abattage* also did a landside business. The hot-to-trot Cointré wrote that she and her partner turned 170 tricks a day at the Panier Fleuri. According to her rough calculation, *les noirs* orgasmed in a mere seven minutes; Caucasian GIs needed an additional three minutes.

The Allied incursion of Paris in some ways was more destabilizing than the Black Years when it came to sex trafficking. The destitute city became a prime

LEFT: GIs on the *Impasse de Guelma* in Montmartre, 1945

destination for American servicemen on three-day furloughs and young French girls from the provinces. Montmartre was awash in unregulated prostitution. Some of the *occasionalles* worked the streets and cafés for the unvarnished thrill; others hoped fraternization with high-ranking GIs might lead to longtime protection or marriage. Everyone needed money.

The Yanks slowly accommodated themselves to the loony spectacle. They referred to Pigalle as "Pig Alley" and attempted to dodge its venereal consequences whenever possible. (The rates of syphilis and gonorrhea among the hard-faced *marcheuses* were astronomical.) According to some GIs, the hourly hotel rooms exactly resembled the disgusting sets created by Hollywood craftsmen for Army hygiene films.

To prevent price gouging, an American Army agency opened four exclusive nightclubs in Paris. The places were mammoth and the Champagne dirt cheap at four dollars a bottle. Only uniformed soldiers and their civilian dates or WACs were permitted inside. The stage entertainment varied from week to week but

ABOVE: *For You* (June 21, 1945)

RIGHT: A MP at *La Guinguette*, 1945

BELOW: *Mad*, *Farewell to Our GI Friends*, 1947

OPPOSITE: John Ingliss Atkinson, *Broadway Tattler*, 1933

the high point was always Hit Parade favorites sung by French chanteuses and discreetly attired lines of chorus dancers. Here was a bit of chaste Americana far from the sleazy surroundings and raging battles.

The American Expeditionary Army remained in Paris long after the unconditional German surrender in May 1945. In fact, GIs were stationed there until the Marshall Plan was announced in early 1947. The vast majority of Parisians hailed their departure. But the unfettered metropolis had already undergone a radical transformation. ⚜

Un cachet
DE 25 CIGUES

L'HÉTAÏRE

MADAME RICHARD'S CRUSADE

*The time has come to embark on the path of purity
and moral regeneration.*

— Marthe Richard, "Declaration to the City Council," 1945 —

*The foundation of a thousand years of civilization
is about to be destroyed.*

— Pierre Mac Orlan to the Editor of *Le Crapouillot* (October 6, 1946) —

ABOLITION

IN FRANCE, THE MOVEMENT TO BAN legalized prostitution had its share of noteworthy activists but little popular support. In the decades before the Great War, abolitionist groups allied themselves with temperance and suffragette societies. These associations were largely derided as Anglo-Saxon fronts, laughable moral campaigns to deprive French men and women of their unique hedonist freedoms.

OPPOSITE: Van Elsen, *The Whore*

ABOVE: Comic photo of Marthe Richard, circa 1948

RIGHT: The Final Morning: October 14th, 1946

The Catholic Church and the major political parties exempted themselves from the debate about public virtue. After all, the criminalization of commercial sex was also an attack on economic liberty and the centrality of pleasure in French culture. Next might be civic constraints on tobacco, unhealthy foodstuffs, or alcohol.

In the 1920s, the war on prostitution in France found a more enduring and firmer transnational grounding. Both revolutionary Soviet Union and Fascist Italy had outlawed sex trafficking as a deleterious bourgeois enterprise. Brothel owners and pimps mentally — and sometimes physically — enslaved underclass women and the intimate burlesque demeaned the sanctity of marital relations. Prostitution also eroded the nation's vitality — indirectly reducing the birth rate, spreading dangerous communicable diseases, and sapping the psychic energies of its participants.

Representatives from the extreme Right and radical Left joined hands with feminist do-gooders to restrict the *maisons closes*. But the *milieu* had its own backers and lobbyists in the National Assembly and city councils. These included powerful sycophants and corrupt officials as well as hundreds of lawmakers, whose silent partnership with the madams was a tabloid joke. Money from the sex *bisnesse* in Paris filled countless pockets. To no one's surprise, every serious attempt to dislodge the industry failed miserably.

THE POSTWAR CRUSADE

The Purge of 1944 and the relentless Yankee quest for French *zigzag* modified libertine views in the recovering state. Yvonne de Gaulle, the Prime Minister's wife, blamed the shuttered houses and Paris' streetwalkers for her country's moral decline. Mme. de Gaulle's animus against legal prostitution was unyielding and somewhat irrational but she had significant encouragement from France's first-time female voters and, better yet, a political alter ego: the spirited sexpot Marthe Richard (1889–1982).

Even by the wacked-out standards of her many eras, Richards' life, in her own telling, achieved epic Victor Hugo-like status. A registered prostitute at sixteen and celebrated love spy in World War I, Richard practically invented the "honey trap." Her first husband, a rich industrialist who taught her to fly, died in the war; her second was the financial director of the Rockefeller Foundation in London. After some stalling, the French government awarded Marthe a Legion of Honor for her "special services" in espionage. The Prime Minister, Édouard Herriot, personally delivered the medallion. He was her current paramour.

The Allied Mata Hari wrote about her wartime exploits in *My Life as a Spy in the French Service.* It went on to become a best-seller in 1936 and the inspiration for a maudlin mainstream feature. Astonishingly, the plucky Richard resumed her undercover activities during the Occupation, palling around with the heads of the Parisian Gestapo. (Haven't they seen the movie?) In 1945, the heroine of two world wars and Christian Democratic candidate was elected to the Municipal Council. She was its only female member.

As the self-appointed "conscience of the new France," Richard rallied against the city's 178 bordellos. She declared, "I will not rest until Paris is cleansed of these stinking sewers, which are a shame to our country and the world!" The ginger-haired reformer denounced them as corrupting and archaic institutions that spawned the VD contagion and moral depravity. Their iniquitous clutch on the French capital was economic as well. The *maisons closes* and their seven thousand sex-workers generated an annual income of one billion *francs,* or twenty million dollars. Much of the legitimate proceeds flowed surreptitiously into law enforcement and the courts, polluting the entire penal system. Marthe

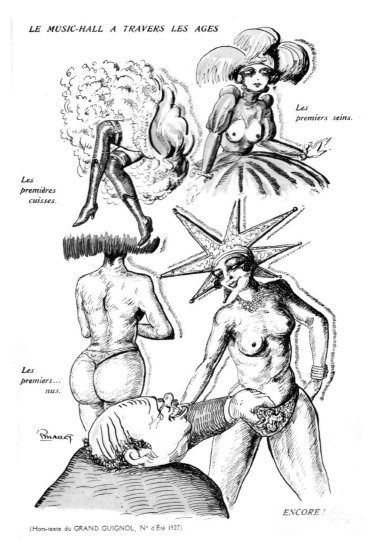

LE MUSIC-HALL A TRAVERS LES AGES

Les premières cuisses.

Les premiers seins.

Les premiers... nus.

ENCORE !

(Hors-texte du GRAND GUIGNOL, N° d'Été 1927)

TOP: P. Mallet, *Music-Hall Through the Ages,* Le Grand Guignol (Summer 1927)

ABOVE: French film, *Marthe Richard, Secret Agent In the Service of France* (1937)

revealed that she had been offered a cool million *francs* to call off her proposed ban but the indefatigable crusader's voice would not be stilled.

On April 13th, 1946, after months of backroom dealing, Richard managed to garner enough votes from her party, the Popular Republican Movement, and the Communists to pass Law No. 46658. It was known as the "Marthe Richard Bill." Police Prefect Charles Luizet announced that the bawdy houses would be out of business by October. Many of the city's Councilmen snuck away from the Chamber in stunned disbelief.

RIGHT: "The Order to Close," (*Le Rire*, 1946)

BELOW: Graffiti outside the Temple of Beauté: "Shit on Marthe Richard," 1946

OPPOSITE LEFT: Jean Dullus, *Useless Mouths to Feed*, 1946

OPPOSITE RIGHT: Furniture and chair sale notice at Le Sphinx, 1946

LA FERMETURE

The official closing of the brothels across France and its Maghreb colonies, or the dreaded *la fermeture*, created endless problems for the various plainclothes vice agencies and their uniformed colleagues. There was an aggregate of 1500 houses and hardly any sympathy for the noble experiment in the French press. The Council's decree was an invitation to madness.

The *maison* owners, once honorable merchants, openly attacked Richard as a demented hypocrite, self-hating loon, or vain publicity hound. They predicted chaos: swarms of medically unchecked *irrégulières* would swell every dim corner of the city; there would be a perplexing upsurge of "gentlemen" rapists; and legions of frustrated Frenchmen would robotically stare at their radio sets. *La belle France* might turn into America! The always quotable Fabienne Jamet sneered, "If the Germans had won the war, our brothels would still be in operation."

DEATH
OF THE
SPHINX

SALUTE (FEB. 1947), SECRETLY PHOTOGRAPHED BY EUGENE KAMMERMAN

LEFT: Removal of furniture and chairs at *Le Sphinx*, 1946

BELOW: Student removing closure notice from the entrance of the *162*, 1946

The day of reckoning fell on October 13th. In the days and weeks that followed, furniture and mementoes from the cathedrals of pleasure were auctioned off. What couldn't be sold or carted away, like the zinc bar counters or pornographic wall tiles, was smashed and dumped in garbage bins. Many of the larger *maisons de rendez-vous* were revamped as school dormitories. The Le Grand 106, that sad slaughterhouse, metamorphosed into an isolated Salvation Army outpost.

In 1952, Marthe Richard reappeared in the French media. The ever protean lass confessed that she had been proved wrong and her detractors were indeed prescient. Streetwalking and venereal disease had skyrocketed over the last five years. In her new book, *The Call of Sex*, Richard pleaded for the reopening of the *maisons de tolérance*. Only this time, the *filles de joie* would have to be better protected and subjected to more rigorous medical inspection.

But the aging hellcat could not turn back the clock. Richard had personally rocked French sex culture to its foundations and no change of heart could undo that. Because of her, she later admitted, Paris stopped being Paris. ✤

MARTRE

DIRECTORY
of
NAUGHTY PARIS
(1930)

~30~
HOTSPOTS

OFFICIAL AND PRIVATE AGENCIES EQUALLY PROMOTED erotic and nighttime activities for adventurous tourists. Below are thirty of the most commonly listed sites. Guidebooks often appended coy or disingenuous warnings to their salacious descriptions. Of course, that did little to dispel curious onlookers or brazen outsiders.

MAISONS de TOLÉRANCE

1T Aux Belles Poules
2T Le Chabanais
3T Le Colbert
4T L'Étoile de Kléber
5T Le Sphinx

MAISONS de SOCIÉTÉ/RENDEZ-VOUS

1S Miss Betty
2S Chez Madame Hélène
3S Maison Denise
4S Au Panier Fleuri
5S Temple de Vénus

MAISONS d'ABATTAGE

1A Le Fort Monjol
2A Moulin Galant

CABARETS, NIGHTCLUBS, and DANCINGS

1C L'Abbaye de Thèléme
2C Le Bouf sur Le Toit
3C Cabaret de l'Enfer
4C Château et Caveau Causcasiens
5C Florida
6C Lido

GAY VENUES

1G Bal des Chiffoniers
2G La Bolée
3G Brasserie Léon
4G Liberty's Bar
5G La Petite Chaumière

LESBIAN VENUES

1L Le Fétiche
2L Le Monocle
3L La Perle

UNDERWORLD DIVES

1U Bal Bousca
2U Chien Qui Fume
3U Grappe d'Or
4U Le Père Tranquille

BROTHELS: MAISONS DE TOLÉRANCE

AUX BELLES POULES 32, Rue Blondel: 1920-46

AREA: 2nd Arrondissement. Above the Porte St. Denis.

ATMOSPHERE: Festive, noisy, filled with smoke.

CLIENTÈLE: Middle-class. Somewhat more urbane after midnight.

"EMPLOYEES": As many as fifty coquettish girls — all under twenty-five years old— crowd the first-level, common area. They mingle with the potential customers, trading jokes, smoking, drinking, and teasingly fondle one another.

EMPLOYER: By the stairway is a desk commandeered by a stern-looking *sous-maîtresse,* who negotiates the transactions.

ENTERTAINMENT: When the piano player takes a break, a mechanical pianola runs nonstop. Prostitutes normally dance with individual customers or play nonsensical card games before climbing the stairs for sexual encounters.

FOOD: Mostly mandatory, overpriced drinks, like cherries in brandy. A stable of naked, middle-aged hostesses refill clients' empty glasses with remarkable speed.

TOURISTS: A must-see attraction for thrill-seeking Americans, Germans, and Russians. French and pidgin English are spoken here.

VARIANT NAMES: Old-timers called this *Le Poplaville,* or the Henhouse.

LE CHABANAIS 12, rue Chabanais: 1878-1946

AREA: 2nd Arrondissement. Around the corner from the Bibliothèque Nationale.

ATMOSPHERE: Aristocratic, extremely exclusive, regal. Polished doors open exactly at midnight.

CLIENTÈLE: Royalty, foreign heads of state, robber

barons from abroad, moneyed *bons vivants*, and Hollywood film stars.

DÉCOR: Shockingly opulent from its nineteenth-century entrance hall (in the form of reconstructed stone manor-corridor) to five floors of lavish theme bedrooms.

"EMPLOYEES": In the plush Selection Salon, normally only four or five ladies are seated at any one time. Each is a different type (typically a Senegalese, a Dutch woman, a Jewess, a naïve provincial, and a sophisticated Parisian).

EMPLOYER: Madame Kelly, the Chab's founder, personally introduces the courtesan-attired young women.

ENTERTAINMENT: Small talk in the sitting room.

FOOD: Fancy appetizers and Mumm Cordon Rouge Champagne.

TOURISTS: Only patrons who have been vetted by the *sous-maîtresse* or obvious celebrities are permitted inside. By 1938, nearly one-third of all Anglo-Saxon sex tourists — half of whom brought spouses — visited this establishment.

LE COLBERT 8, rue Colbert: 1892–1946

AREA: 2ʳᵈ Arrondissement. One block from the Opéra.

ATMOSPHERE: Luxurious.

CLIENTÈLE: Many male film stars and directors, local captains of industry, assorted tycoons, and silk manufacturers from Lyons.

DÉCOR: The Crystal Palace Room has a glass dance floor that is illuminated by underground lighting and a crystal chandelier. Upstairs theme rooms include a Chinese salon; a large Turkish-Harem Room; Persian salon; the Virgin Room with lace curtains and wedding night accoutrements; the Desert Tent Pavilion, centered with piles of carpets; a Chamber of Mirrors, for masochists or sadists, that is furnished with an enormous fireplace complete with paper flames and a wooden crucifix; and a Black Museum, decorated with original erotic art from Asia and Beardsley drawings.

"EMPLOYEES": Thirty young charges dressed in Greco-Roman attire — two of every nationality — are displayed in a semi-circle around the sofas of seated customers.

EMPLOYER: A grumpy *mondaine* with "a face that could nauseate a mother and a voice that could scare fight fans stiff" presents the stable of girls by clapping her manly hands.

ENTERTAINMENT: There is a separate room for the *tableaux vivants*. The ten-minute show has the *femmes* arranged in seductive poses that change every few minutes.

TOURISTS: German, Spanish, and English are widely spoken here.

UNUSUAL: Famous for its Chamber of Mirrors: a dank downstairs compartment stocked with medieval meat hooks, a rack, chains, birch rods, cat-o'-nine-tails, riding crops, bull whips, a white folded cross, wire lattices and metal cuffs.

L'ÉTOILE DE KLÉBER 4, rue Villejust: 1941–46

AREA: 16th Arrondissement. Respectable Right Bank neighborhood.

ATMOSPHERE: Like a hush-hush party at a private art gallery. Regulars refer to it as "The Diplomats' Brothel," or even more discreetly, "The Diplomat."

CLIENTÈLE: Assorted government dignitaries, French movie stars, Sorbonne academics, wealthy Americans couples, and industrialists, all decked out in evening clothes. Especially attractive to affluent types with pronounced perverse tastes, including

humiliating scatological scenes. (Average fee in 1946 is around $500 per session.)

DÉCOR: The main room, known as "the Garden," is filled with lush potted plants and Louis XV chairs, like a Tiffany's showroom or fashionable café on the Champs-Élysées. Six rooms with mirrored ceilings are designated as "peepshows" and have narrow slits in the walls. There, voyeurs (mostly wives or trios of unattached women in bejeweled gowns) can watch unsuspecting customers engage in sexual activity.

"EMPLOYEES": Every variety of prostitute: leggy college coeds, naked Swiss midgets, duos of Amazon-sized Asians in cheongsam dresses or harem trousers, small-time blonde Swedish actresses, pimply-faced French teenagers. Most are replaced every six months. An unlikely in-demand choice is a flat-chested, pale-faced, pince-nez-toting, British gentlewoman.

EMPLOYER: Madame Billy or Brigitte (née Aline Soccodato) runs the house. She is famously remembered for her advice to a prostitute who objected to a

customer who wanted to lap up her feces on a silver plate: "Here, the client is king!"

ENTERTAINMENT: One gambling room with a roulette wheel; another has a string quartet playing a set repertoire of classic music.

FOOD: Caviar plates, fine cognacs, Scotch, and Champagne cocktails (for the girls). Pastries come from Maxim's kitchen.

TOURISTS: Few. Not advertised in the standard brothel guides.

LE SPHINX 31, boulevard Edgar-Quinet: 1931–46

AREA: 14th Arrondissement. In the heart of Montparnasse.

ATMOSPHERE: Upscale, freethinking, avant-garde. Girls in scanty white or red Egyptian costumes sit in two rows of small stools by the entrance.

CLIENTÈLE: A favorite haunt for the hyper-chic and Montparnasse artists, like Alberto Giacometti. Many homosexuals and lesbians on the lookout for openhearted indeterminates. Entire families are welcomed, especially children who are directed to an American-style playroom, which is filled with toys and picture books.

DÉCOR: Hollywood Moderne. A bas-relief of a Sphinx, the symbol of the establishment, faces the street.

"EMPLOYEES": One hundred and twenty *pensionnaires* domicile here. Mostly wholesome Parisian types

— pretty, quick-witted, and independent. One beloved male dwarf works as a servant and jack-of-all-trades.

EMPLOYER: Jointly owned by Charles Martel and the Marseille underworld chieftains. Martel entrusts the day-to-day stewardship to Georges Lemestre and his wife, Marthe.

ENTERTAINMENT: Pornographic films, occasional erotic scenes. Some of the girls are budding *chanteuses*.

FOOD: Fine dining, Taittinger Champagne, the usual. Purchases of bottles of wine and exorbitantly priced cocktails are *de rigueur* for the sexually lackluster.

TOURISTS: Many English and German speakers. Busloads of irritating curiosity-seekers, nicknamed "apple carts," scout out the place for less than an hour and then leave in a swoop.

BROTHELS: MAISONS DE SOCIÉTÉ/ MAISONS DE RENDEZ-VOUS

MISS BETTY 36, rue Saint-Sulpice: 1927–46

AREA: 6th Arrondissement. Facing the Saint-Sulpice Cathedral.

ATMOSPHERE: "Worldly Relations." Mockingly sophisticated. Quiet as a provincial confession booth.

CLIENTÈLE: Clergymen and curious S/M aficionados.

DÉCOR: Clients must negotiate a narrow passage, up a staircase, between two sets of bookshelves jammed with yellowing, leather-bound Catholic missals. Rooms are made up like bedrooms in a cloister.

"EMPLOYEES": One half-dozen "specialists" dressed as nuns or Mother Superiors. Typically, the priests, monks, or lesser-ordained customers begin their "worship" at the foot of the prostitutes' beds and move upward.

ENTERTAINMENT: Hardly any precoital talk.

FOOD: Wine, not the sacred kind.

TOURISTS: Foreign clergy, in-the-know or misplaced travelers.

UNUSUAL: Everything. An enduring venue and subject matter for brothel and anticlerical folklore.

CHEZ MADAME HÉLÈNE 28, rue Brey: 1925-37

AREA: 17th Arrondissement. Two blocks north of the Arc de Triomphe.

ATMOSPHERE: Wild and party-like. Itinerant fun. Every glittering room and floor has a different exciting buzz. Gaiety is the order of the day.

CLIENTÈLE: *Bons vivants* and merrymakers from various walks of Paris' mercantile community.

DÉCOR: Three adjacent buildings, clustered cozily side by side: a sumptuous baroque salon with second-floor studio rooms; a bright, oversized dance hall; and a pitch-black reception chamber, where bemasked clients can mingle with the help.

"EMPLOYEES": Fifty to sixty women dressed in jazz-age finery: low-cut dresses, heavily carmined faces, bobbed hair. Many slim teenager hookers but also older women, painted and powdered to look like debutantes or society chaperons. Flapperish hostesses and a naked Senegalese maid.

EMPLOYER: The bleached-blonde Madame Hélène, who guides the proceedings, is extremely busty and has the thick-set body of a sailor's wife.

ENTERTAINMENT: Besides dancing to a live jazz band or a string quartet, there is a Virgin Peep Show, which costs forty *francs* (in 1933). Clients can gaze through peepholes at a gorgeous blonde who engagingly displays her perfect body, starting with her graceful legs and ending with her gilded nipples. Also, there is an interactive, erotic masquerade in a closed-off compartment that leads to a series of antechambers.

TOURISTS: Flashy foreigners and journalists in the pursuit of "true" French culture.

UNUSUAL: This is yet another favorite hangout for vice officers from Paris' celebrated *Service des Mœurs*. One of the several signs in the Salon warns, "We are not dogs; so do not bite!"

MAISON DENISE 10, rue Papillon: 1923-37

AREA: 9th Arrondissement. South of Pigalle, near Square Montholon.

ATMOSPHERE: At first stately, resembling an Empire drawing room. Quickly it becomes clear that this is a place for extreme perversion. Advertised as the "House of Shudders."

CLIENTÈLE: Moneyed masochists, melancholics, and tradition-bound Catholics.

DÉCOR: In one corner of the reception room is a palm tree and a player piano that pumps out Grieg melodies. Another corner is an exact replica of a harem scheme from a celebrated Beirut brothel, called the *"1001 Nights."*

"EMPLOYEES": Twelve beautiful girls are decked out like backstage ballerinas from a Turkish ballroom scene or elegant priestesses from Sappho's court. The *filles* are chosen for their sadist temperament and

ability to administer savage beatings to their customers' rigid buttocks.

ENTERTAINMENT: The girls enact playful whipping pantomimes on a small stage — promoted as *visions d'art* — such as "The Marvels of Dama" or the "Palace of Califes and Its Beauties." Then they offer the same service to spectators in private rooms.

FOOD: Mimosas, drinks with cassis, fanciful soufflés.

TOURISTS: Many, including American newspapermen, from word-of-mouth recommendations.

AU PANIER FLEURI 17, rue la Huchette: 1923-46

AREA: 6th Arrondissement. Latin Quarter. Just east of Boulevard Saint Michel.

ATMOSPHERE: Neighborly.

CLIENTÈLE: Small-time merchants, local clerks, a few affluent walk-ins — most are old-time customers.

DÉCOR: Each room has a name and function, like the Oriental Chamber; the Schoolroom (with tiny desks and a blackboard); the Blue Chamber; the Red Suite (a Peepshow room); and "the Chamber of Detached Divertissement," a closet from which one could secretly watch the goings-on in the Red Suite while sitting in an armchair.

"EMPLOYEES": The normal "League of Nations" assemblage in miniature: the fat woman; two petite "schoolgirls"; a coal-black doll from Martinique; the "Bride" (a thin Spanish girl dressed in a white Castilian wedding gown and white gloves); a provincial pregnant teen; the Swede, who dyes her hair a pale green and dresses in a similar colored, transparent raincoat; the boyish brunette; the disfigured matron; as well as two masochistic types who like to be whipped (the portly hag and the tough femme).

EMPLOYER: Madame Mariette greets each guest by name and accompanies him into the small, red triangular Selection Parlor.

ENTERTAINMENT: In the front parlor if the mood unexpectedly plummets, some of the girls pound the keys of the out-of-tune, ornate piano and make up lewd renditions of music-hall ditties. Upstairs is a separate room for viewing pornographic films and another soundproof salon for intimate flagellation shows.

TOURISTS: None.

TEMPLE DE VÉNUS
7, rue de la Grange-Batelière: 1925–46

AREA: 9th Arrondissement.

ATMOSPHERE: Perversion is the norm here, moderated by extreme decorum.

CLIENTÈLE: Riff-raff, masochistic gentlemen, unpublished poets, high-ranking senators. Occasional couples who require the watchful eye of a prostitute to achieve full and sustained orgasm.

DÉCOR: Three floors of theme rooms, like the Italian Salle, several lavish Royal Chambers, and eight bathhouses. Two Chambers of Torture can be found in the basement.

"EMPLOYEES": Hardened, if adventurous, streetwalkers and innocent provincial twenty-age-olds. Both groups are schooled in the arts of domination and demonic roleplay. Beatings are usually administered by trios of laughing *dominatrices*.

EMPLOYER: While the customer negotiates with Madame Louise, the proprietor, Maurice Jalabert, sings popular chansons or arias from *La Traviata* to the accompaniment of a teakwood record player. (One writer thought this is the most sadistic aspect of the S/M chateau.)

TOURISTS: Only provincials. Some Germans.

UNUSUAL: Good place for scatological, especially urine imbibing, scenes and femme-on-femme flagellation shows.

BROTHELS:
MAISONS D'ABATTAGE

LE FORT MONJOL 120, rue Monjol: 1922–26

AREA: 19th Arrondissement. To the right of the Métro Combat in Belleville, a decaying neighborhood of abandoned barns, unkempt stables, irregular constructions, and weed-encrusted alleyways. East of everything.

ATMOSPHERE: Sordid, dingy, and reeking of desperation. This somber place radiates evil and "sinister beauty."

CLIENTÈLE: Unemployed stevedores, hopeless drunks, purveyors of the low Belleville nightspots.

DÉCOR: Outside of a dilapidated cul-de-sac, a fantastic staircase leads to a mysterious square, the cobble-stoned ruins of Fort Monjol. Each of the dozen windowless rooms is illuminated with a petrol lamp that conceals the deformed features of the wretched girls.

"EMPLOYEES": Twenty down-and-out whores dressed in Indian yellow, pink, or red East African gowns. Many of the girls have been summarily dismissed from other *maisons closes* or condemned as unsightly lepers.

EMPLOYER: The house procurers work in local cabarets or at municipal residential clinics for lepers.

ENTERTAINMENT: Some of hostesses manage to belt out melancholic refrains from old street ballads.

FOOD: Huh?

TOURISTS: A few gawkers, enthralled by sensational warnings posted in Pigalle guidebooks.

MOULIN GALANT 10, rue de Fourcy: 1922–46

AREA: 4th Arrondissement. Quartier Saint-Paul, a dismal slum area a few blocks north of the Seine.

ATMOSPHERE: "A descent into Hell." Fast, cheap, and a hygienic nightmare.

CLIENTÈLE: Mostly North African workers but also postal clerks, Chinese merchants, garage mechanics, Algerian carpet salesmen, petit bourgeois and blue-collar types. On payday Fridays, they queue up on the Rue de Fourcy pavement and patiently wait their turn.

DÉCOR: On the ground level are two large boxy assembly rooms. The clients line up in the left chamber and the girls in the other. In the middle is a steep staircase, which the assigned couples climb to an upper-floor bank of twenty-two mattressed cubicles.

"EMPLOYEES": Fifty-some women from Eastern Europe. They are mostly naked, except for the scarred ones who cover their wounds or incisions with red satin kimonos.

EMPLOYER: Madame Paulette. On her table is a cash register, where she accepts the fees and issues tickets. Paulette initiates each transaction with a carnival barker's harangue, "The money goes here!"

FOOD: Beer available at a bar but few takers.

TOURISTS: Nary a one.

CABARETS, NIGHTCLUBS, AND DANCINGS

L'ABBAYE DE THÈLÉME 1, place Pigalle: 1885–1934

AREA: 9th Arrondissement. Center of Montmartre.

ATMOSPHERE: *Très chic*.

CLIENTÈLE: Habitat of American millionaires, high rollers, theatre investors, and international procurers. Gorgeously dressed women with their Russian gigolos. Tuxedo-clad Sûreté officers engagingly mingle with the chieftains of *Le Milieu*.

DÉCOR: Glittering entertainment establishment.

ENTERTAINMENT: Black buck-and-winger dancers high-step it before a frantic jazz orchestra. Rhythm-depraved couples attempt to follow suit. Also there are red-coated Hungarian fiddlers, who play Gypsy music, moving from table to table. (No clapping. Only finger-snapping is encouraged.)

EROTIC ENTICEMENT: "Pimp Central." A hotbed of fashion-conscious *poules*, *cocottes*, and *souteneurs*.

LE BŒUF SUR LE TOIT 28, rue Boissy d'Anglais: 1924-28/26; rue de Penthièvre: 1928-36/45; avenue Pierre Ist-de-Serbie: 1936-41/34; rue de Colisée: 1941-46

AREA: 8th Arrondissement. Just around the corner from the Madeleine Church. (Later, south of the Avenue des Champs Elysées.)

ATMOSPHERE: Pleasant, up-to-date, art-filled. Everyone of significance in Bohemia can meet with like-minded artists and their devotees.

CLIENTÈLE: Rendezvous of Montparnasse's super-sophisticated avant-garde. Publishers, Surrealist poets, elegant queers, and businessmen in the know.

DÉCOR: Picasso's painting of an enormous eye, *L'Œil Cacodylate*, overshadows the welcoming dining room and dance floor. Francis Picabia's paintings and Man Ray photographs pasted everywhere between mirrors and gold braiding. Placards from Cocteau's stage productions are hung from hooks.

ENTERTAINMENT: Real black American jazz band plays loud and incessantly between 10 p.m. and 2 a.m.

EROTIC ENTICEMENT: Kiki and Mistinguett's legs. (Once to shock a self-contented businessman and his mistress at the packed bar, Cocteau stuck his head between them and ordered "A shot of freshly ejaculated sperm," which caused a mass walk-out.)

FOOD: Excellent dining — caviar, *foie gras* in pastry, roast duck, and white wines from the Alsace.

CABARET DE L'ENFER
53, boulevard de Clichy: 1896-1946

AREA: 9th Arrondissement. Naturally, in the center of Montmartre.

ATMOSPHERE: Framed with a gaping Hell's Mouth. A doorman dressed like an impish devil waves in potential clients (for 1.25 *francs*). By his side is a placard that proclaims the temperature within this Inferno. The pace indoors is fast-moving and madly frantic.

CLIENTÈLE: Anglo-Saxon tourists mostly.

DÉCOR: An enormous bubbling caldron welcomes the guests to the depths of Purgatory on the ground floor. From a maze of cavern-like walls, thick clouds of smoke and crackling flames erupt. Snakes and serpents, pulled by strings, twist over the heads of the diners.

ENTERTAINMENT: A Gypsy band of male and female musicians bang out selections from *Faust* on guitars while devils prod the recalcitrant music-makers with tridents. After a black-mustached Mephisto and Lucifer roundly insult the diners, they are directed up a stairway to *la Chaudière*, or the "Hot Chamber."

EROTIC ENTICEMENT: On the first floor, Satan introduces the audience to Titania, his diabolic spouse. He tightly binds her to a pillar and spreads hell-fire around her feet. While a nimble red imp and a white-gowned Pierrot contort around the post, Titania is completely consumed in the flames. As soon as the smoke clears, a young female spectator is asked to repeat the auto-da-fé. But moments after the "eternally damned" *femme* is tied to the stake, the volunteer appears totally naked (through an optical illusion) and remains that way until the laughter ceases.

UNUSUAL: *La Chaudière* is actually the chilliest place in the manor.

CHÂTEAU ET CAVEAU CAUCASIENS
54, rue Pigalle: 1923-44

AREA: 9th Arrondissement. Montmartre Headquarters.

ATMOSPHERE: "The mysterious charm of Old Russia" but in an orgiastic Rasputin mode. Things really get started at one o'clock.

CLIENTÈLE: Many partygoing foreigners, especially free-spending Germans, Grand Duchesses, officers from the Imperial Guard, and other such prewar royalty.

DÉCOR: Beautiful three-floor environment, decorated with Central Asian tapestries and Russian exotica. Downstairs is the "rustic cave" with candle-lit tables and a Gypsy band. The *château*, a lavish restaurant and dancing space, has two Russian and American bars. A cabaret and lounge on top.

ENTERTAINMENT: Know-it-all orchestra conductor switches from Tchaikovsky to jazz to Liszt in a beat. Miniature Caucasian dance acts, choral presentations, and balalaika bands. Cossack entertainers, including five authentic Russian princes, perform melancholy Gypsy songs from the Volga or flamboyant sword-balancing *kazatkas*.

EROTIC ENTICEMENT: A fortress of glittering *femmes de restaurant* circulate. Hired Russian *mannequins* dressed as nineteenth-century servant girls bat eyelashes at unsuspecting foreigners and pull chairs up to their tables.

FOOD: Pricey Russian hors d'œuvre dishes and the finest wines and dubious Champagne. Outrageously expensive dishes of biscuits, dates, and salted almonds are brought to the tables unordered. Gratuity taxes and entertainment fees are then added to the bill.

FLORIDA 20, rue de Clichy: 1926-46

AREA: 9th Arrondissement. Lower Montmartre. A five-minute walk to the Pigalle Mètro.

ATMOSPHERE: Most original *dancings* in Paris. Open all night, beginning at 11:30.

CLIENTÈLE: The haunt of the best-groomed and most dashing Argentine bachelors and their diamond-studded girlfriends, *Die-Hards*, American film stars, and the scallywags of the British colony. In season, filled with Paris elite society.

DÉCOR: Pampas decorations in vivid gold and glistening colors, irradiated from an electrified glass dance-floor. At one end of the room is an enormous swimming pool.

ENTERTAINMENT: Canaro's Tango Orchestra from Argentina and Jack Raymond's French jazz band.

EROTIC ENTICEMENT: *Taxi-girls* and *taxi-boys* are available for dancing and sexual companionship. Sprawled around the water tank are six flapperish "mermaids" with pasted-on smiles.

FOOD: Top-dollar *fizz*.

LIDO 78, avenue des Champs Élysées 1925-46

AREA: 8th Arrondissement. In the very center of the Champs-Élysées.

ATMOSPHERE: A mash-up of French tang and American

pacing. "Nothing Like It in the World. A Midnight Babylon."

CLIENTÈLE: Exclusive. Many foreigners.

DÉCOR: A purple and gold Venetian palazzo over an immense underground marble arcade. Twenty fountains at the end of the vast pool spray at intervals.

ENTERTAINMENT: Neapolitan guitar band for tea dancing between ten and eleven. Extravagant naked revues with themes like "Venetian Hours" or "And Voilà Paris." Synchronized swimmers dive and paddle around a gondola, floating in the pool. Beautiful chorines and showgirls.

EROTIC ENTICEMENT: Rouged patrons, wearing revealing, *haute couture* swimsuits, dip into the warm pool as they sip their drinks — among the appreciative rubber horses and duckies.

FOOD: Dinners in trellised garden enclosures.

GAY VENUES

BAL DES CHIFFONIERS
4, rue de Lappe: 1924–1930

AREA: 11th Arrondissement. Near the Bastille.

ATMOSPHERE: Loud and packed with horny males in the relentless pursuit of one-night stands.

CLIENTÈLE: A mix of sailors; Africans in archaic French garb; rouged, muscle-bound men; teenage hustlers in tight-fitting jackets; and quivering, white-haired gay men.

DÉCOR: A mauve-colored room,

bathed in a blaze of overhead lights.

ENTERTAINMENT: Simple *bal-musette* band for *dancings*.

EROTIC ENTICEMENT: Cheek-to-cheek waltzes and a hub for pickups and hashish-laced cigarettes.

LA BOLÉE 25, rue de l'Hirondelle: 1875–1946

AREA: 8th Arrondissement. Latin Quarter. Near the Saint-Michel Mètro.

ATMOSPHERE: Very popular despite (or because of) its cramped quarters and off-putting amusements. The droll Bohemian mood is pretty much set by the *maître d'hôtel*, who greets his guests with the following introduction, "Watch your heads! Then pick any table, my friends. Perhaps the Cuckolded Bench? Or the Table for Idiots? Maybe the one for the Chronically Constipated? Oh, careful, that is the stool for the Intelligent Spectator! It is always empty."

CLIENTÈLE: "The cenacle for fairies" looking for inexpensive fare. Left Bank poets and sketch artists. "A motley public of unknowns."

DÉCOR: The picturesque cellar. The front ceiling is so low that most patrons have to lower their heads to enter. Slapdash art and paintings scattered about.

ENTERTAINMENT: A *bal-musette* orchestra that plays from nine to midnight. Cabaret consists of wacky poetic declamations and comic insults.

EROTIC ENTICEMENT: Perfect spot to organize gay *partouzes*.

FOOD: House specialty is Cherries in Brandy (*cerises à l'eau-de-vie*).

UNUSUAL: Unfortunately for Latin Quartier *pédés*, this *Caveau* in the thirties increasingly attracted a mainstream audience and was reduced to being a featured stop on the what-to-do-after-midnight tourist itinerary.

BRASSERIE LÉON
76, boulevard de Clichy: 1916–36

AREA: 18th Arrondissement. Pigalle.

ATMOSPHERE: *Très privé.* Monsieur Alec, the blonde doorman, has strict orders to weed out undercover *agents des mœurs*, *tantes*, and inquisitive straights. Need a password to enter.

CLIENTÈLE: Good-looking, respectable queers, including Spanish royalty and elderly High Society types, like well-dressed bankers and government officials. Some tight-lipped British financiers on the downlow. "Most elegant inverts in Paris." Only masculine types and their guests. No women allowed.

DÉCOR: Cross between British Men's Club and French *Moderne.*

ENTERTAINMENT: Hot dancing and circumspect mingling.

EROTIC ENTICEMENT: An establishment to bring towel-boys and bellhops without fear of swishy dramatics or public exposure.

FOOD: Recommended drinks: anise-flavored *amourettes* and potent sherry flips.

UNUSUAL: Opium can be purchased in the WC. (But do it on the sly.)

LIBERTY'S BAR 5, place Blanche: 1907–46

AREA: 9th Arrondissement. Smack in Pigalle, across from *the Moulin Rouge Music-Hall.*

ATMOSPHERE: This has a cheerful, smoky Gallic ambiance. Bright welcoming sign in front.

CLIENTÈLE: Gay men and lesbians out for an extended laugh and good food. Some tourists and provincials, cradling guidebooks in their laps.

DÉCOR: Many famous paintings adorn the wall, including some by Jean Cocteau.

ENTERTAINMENT: A five-hour kaleidoscopic show of gay headliners, parody dances, and frivolous songs.

EROTIC ENTICEMENT: Great pickup place for gay encounters. Much bartering between the nutty spectrum of prostitutes and their intended victims.

LA PETITE CHAUMIÈRE
2, rue Berthe: 1922–31

AREA: 18th Arrondissement. On a steep, torturous slope, leading to the top of Montmartre.

ATMOSPHERE: A wizened tiny doorman, dolled up in rouge and wearing a kilt, welcomes the guests. Inside, a "zoo" of self-styled *travestis* in an array of female outfits and prim *frappes.*

CLIENTÈLE: Scarlet-faced merchants, anxious senators, and not so fashionable *lopettes* on the sides. Big-eyed Belgian queers at the bar. Some straight tourists but they don't stay long.

DÉCOR: Cubist paintings, including one of two lanky gentlemen shaking hands over a skull, adorn the room. The dance floor is bathed in a murky pinkish glow.

ENTERTAINMENT: An amateurish cabaret show that features line dances and miniature ballets. Flamboyant couples on the door floor who are covered in feathers and boas or decked out as hairy-chested *apaches.* Many sport artificial rubber breasts.

EROTIC ENTICEMENT: Teams of *roberts* and *minettes*, looking to make an easy twenty-five or thirty-franc score. A private, red-plush, and airless love nest one floor above the cabaret can be secured.

FOOD: Serious drinking along with illicit drugs. Bare-chested waitresses serve inferior Champagne.

LESBIAN VENUES

Elle et...   *Eux...*

LE FÉTICHE 32, rue Fontaine: 1923–44

AREA: 9th Arrondissement. Montmartre, Montmartre.

ATMOSPHERE: Animated. "Educational" for the hets.

CLIENTÈLE: Smug *gousses* in dinner jackets and their smashing femme dates. Many bisexual women and smooth-skinned mulattos. Straight artists are among the *Fétiche's* weekly habitués.

DÉCOR: Roses are the emblems of the place — either sketched on the blank wall-spaces or as electric roses wrapped around trellises.

ENTERTAINMENT: A supremely talented one-man orchestra bangs out every instrument for lesbian social dances, especially raunchy foxtrots and tangos. (Licensing problems have limited the number of musicians.)

EROTIC ENTICEMENT: All femmes are fair game within the premises for the on-the-prowl butches. This includes the overdressed straight wives.

FOOD: Biological female waiters and a barkeep but address them as *garçons*.

LE MONOCLE 60, boulevard Edgar-Quinet: 1932–46

AREA: 14th Arrondissement. In the shadow of the Montparnasse Cemetery.

ATMOSPHERE: Hard-drinking and hard-partying crowd until five in the morning.

CLIENTÈLE: Here spiffy deep-voiced women (*gouines*)

dance with more high-pitched-speaking women (*mannequins*). Haute-fashioned patrons in slicked-back hairstyles and monocles. Many bring their poodles. Groups of gay men and straight gawkers.

DÉCOR: Wall-sized murals of dancing flappers and *monos* being chased from a meadow. Tiny orchestra stage but plenty of room for sensational tango dancing.

ENTERTAINMENT: Four-piece female band. Lesbian comic numbers aggressively directed by Lulu, a hefty cross-dresser, in her trademarked white straw hat, starched collar, and well-tailored jacket.

EROTIC ENTICEMENT: Novice *amazones* can purchase *gaudmichés*, or dildoes, in the WC.

FOOD: House specialty is the *diabolo*, a sickly-sweet concoction of port and grenadine.

LA PERLE 59, bis rue Pigalle: 1925–1939

AREA: 9th Arrondissement. On the Montmartre strip.

ATMOSPHERE: Wild in the post-midnight hours. Although male curiosity-seekers are sometimes seated in the early evening, many of the hawk-faced regulars stare at them with disdain and palpable contempt.

CLIENTÈLE: Tuxedoed butches or *gigolettes* with their girlfriends in elegant ballroom dresses. Most pairings are between physically mismatched types. Young single women from the *Rive Gauche* in search of outré excitement.

DÉCOR: Arranged like elegant tavern with potted palms and tiny panes of red-shrouded windows.

ENTERTAINMENT: Good place for frivolous dalliances on the crammed dance floor. This is the *lesbienne* HQ for newcomers and pickup *artistes*.

EROTIC ENTICEMENT: Companionship for purchase. Elderly *gousses* can effortlessly rendezvous with cynical, perky-breasted *montmartroises* for late-night escapades.

FOOD: A mandatory ice bucket of Champagne and vase of fresh roses is placed on every table. The overstocked bar does landslide business on weekends. Prices are unlisted and arbitrarily devised by the barkeep according to the alcoholic buoyancy and appearance of the customer.

ENTERTAINMENT: Tangos, javas, Black Bottoms, Charlestons. A three-man orchestra. Between each dance, a big fat Breton woman, with a big leather bag slung over her shoulder, hollers to the dancers to kick in some *centimes*.

EROTIC ENTICEMENT: Dangerous-looking men and women patrol the room, looking for fresh partners. And you have to dance with anyone who asks you. Men often java with other males, women with women.

UNUSUAL: One of the few places to see real *apaches*, especially on Wednesdays, the *milieu's* Sabbath. Usually safe for guests. A sign reads: "No Knife-Fighting, Pistol-Shooting, or Smashing of Teeth."

UNDERWORLD DIVES

BAL BOUSCA 13, rue de Lappe: 1911–46

AREA: 11th Arrondissement. Two blocks north of the Place de la Bastille.

ATMOSPHERE: Horridly loud. Mayhem starts at nine in the evening and ends punctually at midnight, when the customers begin their nocturnal workday. Uproar of mechanical pianos, banjos, drums, accordions, laughter, handclaps, and boisterous stamping.

CLIENTÈLE: Rue de Lappe *apaches*, wearing their characteristic caps, colorful scarves, and flashy moccasin footwear. Their *gigolettes* are in close attendance. Orderly, yet threatening crowd. (Sometimes fisticuffs are added to the musical scene.) Few outsiders, except for sailors and local blacks.

DÉCOR: Large packed dance hall. Brilliantly lighted. Just a tiny stage for the band. On the walls are oversized depictions of *apache* life.

CHIEN QUI FUME 33, rue du Point-Neuf: 1922–46

AREA: 1st Arrondissement. "In the Belly of Paris," Les Halles.

ATMOSPHERE: A little hellish. Much coming and going. Perfect off-the-path destination for American poseurs.

CLIENTÈLE: Off-duty night workers or laborers preparing for the morning rush: milkmen, waiters, doormen, *forts*, and street cleaners. Unemployed Russians. Fur and tuxedo crowd on the slum. A coterie of unattached prostitutes near the stairwell.

DÉCOR: Ground floor looks like a low wine shop, furnished with a zinc-bar spittoon, and rickety stools. Upstairs is a more elaborate bar, and large dance floor.

ENTERTAINMENT: A sleazy cabaret

show with a lunatic two-man orchestra. Nothing starts before three in the morning.

EROTIC ENTICEMENT: Whores in the morning but you've got to feed them drinks.

FOOD: Plates of oysters, washed down with Alsatian wine. Snails and a delicious stew made from lamb's feet. As the pink dawn creeps into the busy market streets, restorative onion soup is the typical gastronomic conclusion. The *canaille* never stop cajoling *michés* for *crème de menthe au cassis*, their traditional sickly-sweet repast.

GRAPPE D'OR 1, rue Courtalon: 1920–38

AREA: 1st Arrondissement. In an unlighted alley near the Square des Innocents and the Central Markets.

ATMOSPHERE: Known as "the Palace of the *Clochards*." Reeking of sweaty bodies, halitosis, unwashed socks and underwear, garlic, and urine. Opens at six in the evening and, at exactly five in the morning, the *misérables* are ushered out into the street. Dim with mysterious shadows.

CLIENTÈLE: Homeless male and female derelicts, who can pass out on the wooden benches, tabletops, or in piles on the floor for forty *sous* (1928) or the price of a drink. Occasional bohemians and denizens of the *demimonde*.

DÉCOR: Outside a broken window that has been mended with a yellowing newspaper. A bare square room,

like the kind used for discarded merchandise, lighted by a single lamp swinging from the rafters.

ENTERTAINMENT: A view of Purgatory.

EROTIC ENTICEMENT: *Clandestines* on a break.

FOOD: Cheap Alsatian wine by the glass or mugs of *casse-pattes* ("Leg-breakers"), a concentrated wine from Aramon that is said to disable the drinker. Onion soup.

UNUSUAL: The ruthless owner is a wealthy, straitlaced matron who dutifully attends church every Sunday. She mandates, for

propriety's sake, that all the sleeping bums rest their heads on their forearms, rather than directly touch her tables with their foreheads or stretch out supine on the bare floor.

LE PÈRE TRANQUILLE
16, rue Pierre-Lescot: 1909–46

AREA: 1st Arrondissement. Dangerous crime-infested neighborhood. In the center of Les Halles.

ATMOSPHERE: Quaint underworld *bistro*, opens at four o'clock in the morning and stays that way until the eight o'clock market moves into full swing.

CLIENTÈLE: Favorite hangout for *apaches* and their *poules*. Lusty *forts* and solitary drunks. Also a curious crowd of Left Bank poets, as well as artists and their models, in search of a thrill. Sometimes alcoholic American vaudevillians can be found here, secure from the prying eyes of newspaper columnists.

DÉCOR: Spacious upstairs for drinking and dance; rough-and-tumble ground floor for food. Private backroom for private doings.

ENTERTAINMENT: Tiny little orchestra on the first floor.

EROTIC ENTICEMENT: Annoying whores and their *mecs*.

FOOD: Naturally *soupe à l'oignon* with *choucroute*. Best drinks are made with kir and Calvados. ❖

SELECTED BIBLIOGRAPHY

GUIDEBOOKS AND CONTEMPORARY ACCOUNTS

Allons-y!!! Pour les Plaisirs de Paris (Paris: René Bourzac, 1932).

Comment et où s'amuser à Paris (Paris: Les Éditions du Couvre-Feu, 1935).

Guide des Plaisirs à Paris (Paris: Administration, 1928).

Guide-Indicateur des Maisons de Plaisirs et d'Arts de Paris (Paris: Éditions GOF, 1925).

Guide Rose 1933 (Paris: Privately Printed, 1933).

Mantarville, Jacques, *Maisons de Plaisirs: Distractions Parisiennes* (Paris: Librairie Artistique and Édition Parisienne Réunies, 1929).

Montmartre en 1927 (Paris: Éditions Artistiques de Paris, 1928).

Montmartre et ses Plaisirs! (Paris: Administration, 1926).

Paris en 8 Nuits (Paris: Nilsson, 1931).

Valmondois, Jean, *Guide Intime des Plaisirs de Paris et d'Ailleurs* (Paris: Privately Printed, 1937).

Carco, Francis, *Nuits de Paris* (Paris: Le Divan, 1927).

Choisy, Maryse, *A Month Among the Girls* [1928] (New York: Pyramid Books, 1960). Translated by Lawrence Blochman.

Dekobra, Maurice, *Le Sabbat des Caresses* (Paris: Éditions Baudinière 1935).

Geyraud, Pierre, *Les Petites Églises de Paris* (Paris: Êditions Émile-Paul Frères, 1937).

Meslin, Henri, *Théorie et Pratique de la Magie Sexuelle* (Paris: Librairie Astra, 1938).

Roberti, Jacques, *Maisons de Société* (Paris: Artheme Fayard, 1927).

Royer, Louis-Charles, *Let's Go Naked* (New York: Brentano's, 1932). Translated by Paul Quiltana.

Salardenne, Roger, *Le Culte de la Nudité* (Paris: Parma, 1931).

Thimmy, René, *La Magie à Paris* (Paris: Éditions de France, 1934).

Valti, Luc, *Femmes de Cinq Heures* (Paris: Éditions de France, 1930).

Willy, *The Third Sex* [1927] (Urbana and Chicago: University of Illinois Press, 2007]. Translated by Lawrence R. Schehr.

Willy and Pol Prille, *Les Bazars de la Volupté* (Paris: Éditions Montaigne, 1930).

Chancellor, John, *How to Be Happy in Paris Without Being Ruined!* (London: Arrowsmith, 1926).

Day, George, *Pleasure Guide to Paris* (Paris: Fontenay-aux-Roses, 1927).

How to Enjoy Paris (Paris: International Publications, 1926).

Pleasure Guide to Paris: Paris By Day, Paris By Night (Paris: Administration, 1925).

Phillips, Arthur, *The Gay City* (New York: Brentano's, 1925).

Reynolds, Bruce, *Paris With the Lid Lifted* (New York: George Sully & Co., 1927).

Street, Julian, *Where Paris Dines* (Garden City, NY: Doubleday, Doran & Co., 1929).

SELECTED BIBLIOGRAPHY

Vane, Roland, *Night Haunts of Paris* (Hanley, UK: Archer Press, Inc., 1949).

Woon, Basil, *The Paris That's Not in the Guide Books* (New York: Robert M. McBride & Co., 1926).

Abt, Samuel (ed.), *The Paris Edition: the Autobiography of Waverley Root 1927-1934* (San Francisco: North Point Press, 1987).

De Leeuw, Henrik, *Sinful Cities of the Western World* (New York: Citadel Press, 1934).

Gay, Jan, *On Going Naked* (Garden City, NY: Garden City Publishing Co., 1932).

Huddleston, Sisley, *Paris Salons, Cafés, Studios* (New York: Blue Ribbon Books, 1928).

Josephy, Helen and Mary Margaret McBride, *Paris Is A Woman's Town* (NY: Coward-McCann, Inc., 1929).

Merrill, Frances and Mason, *Among the Nudists* (Garden City, New York: Garden City Publishing, 1931).

Neville, Ralph, *Days and Nights in Montmartre and the Latin Quarter* (New York: George H. Doran Co., 1927).

GENERAL HISTORICAL AND SCHOLARLY BOOKS

Alexandrian, Sarane, *Les Libérateurs de l'Amour* (Paris: Éditions du Seuil, 1977).

Allan, Tony, *The Glamour Years: Paris 1919-40* (New York: Gallery Books, 1977).

Bouvet, Vincent and Gérard Durozoi, *Paris 1919-1939* (Paris: Éditions Hazan, 2009).

Buisson, Patrick, *1940-1945 Années érotiques* (Paris: Albin Michel, 2008).

Dubois, Claude, *La Bastoche: Bal-musette, plaisir et crime 1750-1939* (Paris: Editions Dufelin, 1997).

Lucas, Netley, *Criminal Paris* (London: Hurst & Blackett, 1926).

Pryce-Jones, David, *Paris in the Third Reich* (New York: Holt, Rinehart, and Winston, 1981).

Quignard, Marie-Françoise and Raymond-José Seckel, *L'Enfer de la Bibliothèque* (Paris: Bibliothèque Nationale de France, 2008).

Slocombe, George, *Paris in Profile* (Boston & New York: Houghton, Mifflin Co., 1929).

Willemin, Véronique, *La Mondaine: Histoire et archives de la Police des Mœurs* (Paris: Éditions Hoëbeke, 2009).

MEMOIRS AND BIOGRAPHIES

Madame Billy, *La Maîtresse de "Maison"* (Paris: La Table Ronde, 1980).

Brassaï, *The Secret Paris of the '30s* [1976] (London: Thames & Hudson, 2001). Translated by Richard Miller.

Cointré, Marie-Thérèse, *I'm For Hire* [1947-1948] (North Hollywood, CA: Brandon House, 1966).

Jamet, Fabienne, *One Two Two* (Paris: Olivier Orban, 1975).

Koestler, Arthur, *Arrow in the Blue* (New York: Macmillan Co., 1952).

Martoune (Marthe Lemestre), *Madame Sphinx Vous Parle. Souvenirs recueillis par Antoine Giovanni et Michel Trécourt* (Paris: Euredif, 1974).

Paul, Elliot, *The Last Time I Saw Paris* (New York: Random House, 1942).

Peyrefitte, Roger, *Manouche* (New York: Grove Press, 1974). Translated by Sam Flores.

Pluquet, Marc, *La Sophiale. Marie de Naglowska* (Paris: Unpublished Ms., 1981).

Seldes, George, *Witness to a Century* (New York: Ballantine Books, 1987).

Worthington, Marjorie, *The Strange World of Willie Seabrook* (New York: Harcourt, Brace & World, 1966).

DIRECTED STUDIES

Barbedette, Gilles and Michel Carassou, *Paris Gay 1925* (Paris: Presses de la Renaissance, 1981).

Boudard, Alphonse, *La Fermeture* (Paris: Robert Laffont, 1986).

Boudard, Alphonse and Romi, *L'Age D'Or des Maisons Closes* (Paris: Albin Michel, 1990).

Canet, Nicole, *Décors de Bordels 1860-1946* (Paris: Galerie Au Bonheur du Jour, 2011).

——————— *Hôtels Garnis* (Paris: Galerie Au Bonheur du Jour, 2012).

——————— *Maisons Closes Catalogue* (Paris: Galerie Au Bonheur du Jour, 2009).

De Naglowska, Maria, *Le Rire Sacré de l'Amour Magique* (Paris: Privately Printed, 1932).

De Taillac, Pierre, *Les Paradis Artificiels* (Paris: Hugo & Cie, 2007).

Gordon, Mel, *The Grand Guignol: Theatre of Horror and Terror* (New York: Amok Press, 1988).

Latimer, Tirza True, *Women Together/Women Apart* (New Brunswick, NJ and London: Rutgers University Press, 2005).

Lemonier, Marc and Alexandre Dupouy, *Histoire(s) du Paris Libertin* (Paris: La Musardine, 2003).

Lyford, Amy, *Surrealist Masculinites* (Berkeley and Los Angeles: University of California Press, 2007).

Medway, Gareth, *Lure of the Sinister* (New York: New York University Press, 2001).

Pessis, Jacques and Jacques Crépineau, *The Moulin Rouge* (New York: St. Martin's Press, 1990). Translated by Malcolm Hall.

——————— *Les Folies Bergère* (Paris: Fixot, 1990).

Pierre, José (ed.), *Investigating Sex: Surrealist Discussions 1928-1932* (London/New York: Verso, 1992). Translated by Malcolm Imrie.

Roberts, Mary Louise, *What Soldiers Do: Sex and the American GI in World War II France* (Chicago and London: University of Chicago Press, 2013).

Romi, *Maisons Closes* (Paris: Privately Printed, 1952).

Shack, William A., *Harlem in Montmartre* (Berkeley and Los Angeles: University of California Press, 2001).

Teyssier, Paul, *Maisons Closes Parisiennes* (Paris: Parigramme, 2010).

JOURNALS AND MAGAZINES

Beauté, Le Crapouillot, Détective, For You, Frou-Frou, Jazz, Journal Secret, La Madelon, The Night-Light, Paris-Flirt, Paris Music-Hall, Paris Magazine, Paris Plaisirs, Paris Sex-Appeal, Paris Spectacles, Paris Toujours, Pariser Leben, Plaisirs de Paris, Police Magazine, Pour Lire à Deux, Le Rire, Sans-Gene, Séduction, Semaine à Paris, Le Sourire, Témoignages de Notre Temps, La Vie Parisienne, Vive Paris, Voilà, Votre Destin, and *Vu.*

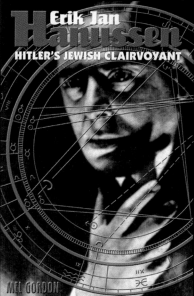

VOLUPTUOUS PANIC: THE EROTIC WORLD OF WEIMAR BERLIN
BY MEL GORDON

A compendium of erotic depravity from the Weimar era, this deluxe paperback edition contains hundreds of rare visual delights from the pre-Nazi, Cabaret-period "Babylon on the Spree," and has the distinction of being praised both by scholars and avatars of contemporary culture, inspiring performers, filmmakers, historians, designers and musicians like the Dresden Dolls and Marilyn Manson. ISBN 9780922915965, PAPERBACK, 8.5 X 11, 300 PAGES, $34.95

ERIK JAN HANUSSEN, HITLER'S JEWISH CLAIRVOYANT
BY MEL GORDON

Erik Jan Hanussen made a name for himself as Europe's most audacious and controversial sooth-sayer. In March 1932, when Adolf Hitler's political future seemed doomed, Hanussen's prediction of a resurgence of the Nazi Party gained him the ear of the superstitious Führer. But what Hitler didn't know initially was that Hanussen was not the Dane he claimed to be but a Jew from Moravia whose given name was Herschel Steinschneider. ISBN 9780922915682, HARDCOVER, 6 X 9, 296 PAGES, $24.95

AMERICAN GROTESQUE: THE LIFE AND ART OF WILLIAM MORTENSEN
EDITED BY LARRY LYTLE AND MICHAEL MOYNIHAN

This stunning compendium reveals the life and work of Hollywood photographer William Mortensen, the unsung pioneer of the "American Grotesque." This book contains a biographical account of Mortensen's life along with his own eloquent manifesto called "Venus & Vulcan." American Grotesque includes over one hundred plates of Mortensen's work, many published here for the first time. ISBN 9781936239979, HARDCOVER, 9 X 12, 300 PAGES, $45.00